30-DAY JOURNEY TO

ACCELERATE YOUR SUCCESS

ACCELERATE

30-DAY JOURNEY TO

YOUR

ELEVATE YOUR PERFORMANCE &
FUEL YOUR PROFESSIONAL GROWTH

SUCCESS

ALYSON VAN HOOSER
PHILLIP VAN HOOSER

Published and distributed by:

SOUND WISDOM
P.O. Box 310
Shippensburg, PA 17257-0310
717-530-2122

info@soundwisdom.com
www.soundwisdom.com

While efforts have been made to verify information contained in this publication, neither the author nor the publisher assumes any responsibility for errors, inaccuracies, or omissions. While this publication is chock-full of useful, practical information; it is not intended to be legal or accounting advice. All readers are advised to seek competent lawyers and accountants to follow laws and regulations that may apply to specific situations. The reader of this publication assumes responsibility for the use of the information. The author and publisher assume no responsibility or liability whatsoever on the behalf of the reader of this publication.

Cover design by Eileen Rockwell
Interior design by Terry Clifton

ISBN 13 TP: 978-1-64095-367-3
ISBN 13 eBook: 978-1-64095-368-0

For Worldwide Distribution, Printed in the U.S.A.
3 4 5 6 7 8 / 25 24 23 22

Contents

Two Generations—One Roadmap to Success

Usually, the first thing people ask is, "What makes this book any different than all the other professional development books out there?" Well, let's get down to it.

This book is written by both a man and a woman—a boomer and a millennial; a father and his daughter-in-law, respectively. These two very different people have come together with a unified position on the knowledge and skills required to earn success in today's radically diverse, rapidly changing world.

Phillip Van Hooser is a Hall of Fame keynote speaker, six-time author, and trusted leadership development advisor to top U.S. companies and entrepreneurs. Phil cut his professional teeth as a human resources professional and for the last 30 years has worked with thousands of people across industries as varied as banking, insurance, manufacturing, mining, energy, and construction. His breadth of experience guiding people to achieve greater results uniquely positions him to share his perspective on the commonsense prerequisites for success.

Alyson Van Hooser is a millennial blazing a path for others to achieve professional success. Growing up in poverty, surviving a home life ravaged by addiction and abuse, Alyson emerged instinctively smarter and with an uncanny ability to connect people with their goals, leaders with their followers, and organizations with their customers. Achieving quick success in the retail, banking, insurance, and government sectors, Alyson has the experience and the expertise to drive individual and team transformation. She has unearthed the roots needed to ground people in success, and her audiences are more resilient and successful because of the principles she shares.

Here's where the power team met...

Phil had a front-row seat to Alyson's early personal and professional growth. Alyson began dating his son when she was just 16 years old. Thirteen years later, when Alyson had more than proven her grit, knowledge, and leadership skills, Phil and Alyson joined forces to take professional development to the next level. What's most interesting is that Alyson herself is a product of Phil's professional development training sessions. When asked why they teamed up, Alyson will unapologetically and enthusiastically tell you every time that it's because the knowledge and skills she learned from Phil and put into action were the X factors to igniting her success. And Phil will say Alyson is a real-life example of what it takes to achieve unimaginable success when you're willing to commit to the goal and work to make it a reality.

Together, Alyson and Phil have discovered that while they may differ on the finishing touches required to achieve success, they agree on the foundation. And that's what they're doing in this book—equipping you with the right building blocks to get your foundation in place. Because of Chip and Jo, we all know that without a solid foundation, the rest of your house (or your career) will fail.

So regardless of your generation, geography, or gender, you're about to embark on a journey that will accelerate your success—if you commit to it. Are you ready? Let's go!

Commit to the Journey

Every day there seems to be another success strategy released into the world, yet so many people are still struggling to figure out how to arrive. Until now.

We want to challenge you—not to do something new, but to do what's tried and true. For 30 days, commit to intentionally focusing on accelerating your success.

These 30 days will demand dedication and endurance. That's the price of admission to success. But your dedication, commitment, and preparation will create a strong foundation that positions you for exponential results.

At some point in this challenge, you may decide you've nailed these principles. At other times, you may believe you're incredibly ill-equipped for the call to success. Either way, put your stake in the ground, and commit to being better than you are today. That is how success happens.

For those who never start or who quit early, regret is the lens that captures their life story. But for those wanting to fuel growth, you'll never regret this work.

So, starting today, we challenge you to begin the journey to accelerate your success.

Your Success Journey Begins

In May 1804, an expedition left St. Louis, Missouri, on a journey of exploration and discovery. For the next 28 months, this hearty band of adventurers endured hardship, peril, and the great unknown, in their singular quest to map a northwest passage to the Pacific Ocean.

In the fall of 1806, the Lewis and Clark Expedition triumphantly returned to share their many findings with U.S. President Thomas Jefferson. Throughout their journey, Meriwether Lewis and William Clark made meticulous daily or weekly entries in personal journals. Their documentation would ultimately provide untold benefit for future pioneers, paving the way for countless others to follow their documented path until confident enough to blaze their own trail.

This book is designed to help you chart your own course so that you can accelerate your performance and success. We'll share valuable lessons from our own explorations of, and journeys to, success. Our experiences and encounters have left indelible marks—guideposts, let's say—on the path to greater success. These lessons have served us well, and we hope they will help you, too.

You don't have to be successful already to benefit. You don't even have to be on the road to success. All that's needed is a burning desire and willingness to work toward getting better.

You'll discover valuable ideas to help you improve relationships, plan and communicate well, cultivate emotional intelligence, work with different kinds of people, take more calculated risks, and create a better work/life balance.

Oh, by the way, there's one other thing.

If you're feeling a little uncertain right now; if you're imagining all the difficulties and unknowns that may lay ahead, just take a minute to imagine yourself in Meriwether Lewis's shoes on the eve of his expedition's departure into the great unknown. From his journal, in his own words:

We were about to penetrate a country at least two thousand miles in width, on which the foot of civilized man had never trod...[yet] the picture which now presented itself to me was a most pleasing one.

Entertaining as I do the most confident hope of succeeding in a voyage which had formed a darling project of mine for the last ten years, I could but esteem this moment of my departure as among the most happy of my life.

This moment—"the most happy of your life"? Probably not.

But this book may be the catalyst to "the most confident hope of succeeding" in your professional journey. We're certainly happy to begin this journey with you! Let's head out!

CATALYST 1

Success

CHAPTER 1

Defining Success

"Success is synonymous with choices."
—PHILLIP VAN HOOSER

A few years ago, I was invited to speak to a group of high school students on the topic of "preparing for professional success." And boy, did I make a big mistake! I actually went in thinking these young people would be interested in what I had to say. Wrong!

I quickly learned that this group was less interested in learning about how to be successful and more interested in learning about how to become rich and famous. Sadly, "fame and fortune" to them was synonymous with "success," and they wrongly assumed I held the keys to the kingdom. In the end, they didn't like what I had to say very much. You might not either.

I'm concerned some professionals might suffer from a similar inclination—the desire to pursue adoring fans and riches over true, sustainable success.

Let's face facts. Over time, the singular desire for "fame and fortune" has been a common temptation that has dogged, even doomed, too many business professionals and team members. In pursuing these elusive traits, too many otherwise capable professionals end up foolishly sacrificing their legitimate opportunity to be successful.

And there's the real quandary of choice: Fame? Fortune? Or success?

Given the choice, the selfish me would always *choose* fortune—but with anonymity.

Yes, you heard right. I said anonymity rather than fame. At this stage in my life, one thing is pretty clear: if you're fortunate enough to be rich, it's far better if no one else knows it!

So here is my definition of success. It's not fame. It's not fortune. My definition of success is—choices!

For me, success is synonymous with choices. Or said a different way: The more choices you have available—personally or professionally—the more successful you are. Conversely, the fewer the choices you have available, the less successful you are. But unquestionably, the worst-case scenario for any of us is having no choices available, specifically because others are making your choices for you.

Rarely a week goes by that I don't hear someone exclaim in a highly exasperated or agitated tone, "I wish I didn't have so many decisions to make. I wish someone would just tell me what to do."

And each time I hear such a statement, I think, *No! No!! NO!!!*

Realize this: If you're in a situation where you're no longer being asked to decide, it's fair to assume you're being told what to do, when to do it, and how it should be done. Guess what? You're no longer in control of your success. More likely, you're following someone else's lead, or maybe you're even being dragged along, kicking and screaming.

To avoid such an unfortunate outcome, my advice is fourfold:

1. Be thankful for every choice available to you—be the choices large or small, difficult or simple. Every choice matters.

2. Prepare yourself to make good, well-informed decisions when the opportunities do present themselves. You can be prepared by "seeking opportunity, not security." The more you learn and know, the better your opportunities to choose and grow.

3. Seek input from others. The deeper the pool of options, the more opportunities to build on your foundation of success.

4. And finally, don't quit. Don't give up. Ever! If or when you quit, it's game over. Future opportunities to choose diminish or cease. And too often, with quitting comes a statement that successful professionals never have to utter: "I wish I had…"

So don't wish you had. Choose for yourself, and define your success.

Ideas to Accelerate My Success

_____

_____

_____

_____

_____

_____

_____

_____

_____

_____

_____

_____

_____

_____

_____

_____

_____

_____

_____

_____

_____

_____

_____

CHAPTER 2

Blow Up Your Tendencies

"Create tendencies that naturally steer you toward success." —ALYSON VAN HOOSER

I branched out of my comfort zone…and with a mouth full of cured meat, I was instantly reminded why my tendency is to eat only food I'm familiar with (or at least can pronounce)!

Typically, every year on our wedding anniversary (New Year's Eve!), Joe and I go out for a really nice dinner— ALONE. We've had four kids in eight years, so dinner alone is a big deal for us.

This particular year, we decided to spend the evening in Nashville. As we sat down to the table we reserved months in advance, I quickly realized this was one of the fanciest restaurants I had ever been in.

You have to know that when it comes to food, I tend to gravitate toward things that come in shades of brown. Yes, brown food. You're probably thinking, "What in the world is 'brown food'?" Picture all the shades of fries, chicken strips, hamburgers, bread, pasta, and soda. That sounds like a toddler's dream menu, right? I'm 32, but I still tend to crave the food I grew up on, right or wrong.

Joe knows this about me—I'm not naturally adventurous when it comes to food. He, on the other hand, will eat and enjoy just about anything. So, knowing full well I was going to order a steak and potato (yummy brown food), he tried to get me to venture out, on the appetizer at least.

With a huge smile on his face and a quick wink to me, I listened as he asked the server for one specific appetizer. I didn't even understand what Joe said when he ordered, but it was our anniversary, so I was going to roll with it.

Minutes later, the server delivered a beautiful platter of artistically placed dried meats and cheeses—a charcuterie board before charcuterie was *all that* like it is today. Without hesitation, Joe said, "You'll like *this*" and popped a fork full of cured red meat in my mouth. And the world stopped turning.

What day is it?! Am I alive?! What is this?! Should I spit it out?! Yes! Wait…! I probably shouldn't because unlike fast food restaurants, you don't throw away these perfectly pressed cloth napkins! Ugh!!

Whew. I started to sweat. My internal monologue was no help in the moment. So, I sat there and chewed it up like an adult. And then…I realized I actually liked it!

My natural tendency toward food choices had served me just fine in my then 29 years, but when I got a taste of something new that I liked, it was a moment of reflection. I could see, just like in this situation, how I could be enjoying better things in life if I'd just be bold enough to get out of my comfort zone.

I've had to blow up that tendency—get rid of it and create a new one—one where I intentionally go outside of my comfort zone.

You know, we all have our own tendencies. Some tendencies are good for us...like the tendency to think before we speak. And then some tendencies just aren't helping us live life to the fullest...whether it's avoiding a new food or a new opportunity. Here are 11 questions to help you understand which tendencies you should blow up so that you can intentionally start creating the ones that lead to greater success.

Evaluate Your Tendencies

1. When things get tough, do I tend to give up, or do I tend to push through?

2. Do I tend to care more about what others say, or do I tend to stick with what I want?

3. Do I tend to sit back, or do I tend to take charge?

4. Do I tend to stay within my comfort zone, or do I tend to take risks?

5. Do I tend to shoot from the hip, or do I tend to fully prepare before making a move?

6. Do I tend to easily get distracted, or do I tend to stay laser focused?

7. Do I tend to put off the work I don't want to do, or do I tend to get that work finished first?

8. What tendencies do I have that help me get closer to the life I want?

9. What tendencies do I have that stand in my way of getting the life I want?

10. What would I want people in my inner circle to say I tend to do?

11. Am I open to considering feedback from others and making necessary changes?

Tend to Succeed

The goal should be to create tendencies that naturally steer you toward success. We're not all geared toward making decisions instinctively to get us there, but we can establish new tendencies. Tendencies are created by habits. Habits can be created by making consistent choices.

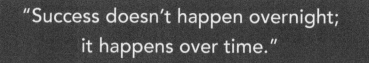

"Success doesn't happen overnight; it happens over time."

For example, after I had my third baby, I wanted to lose weight and get healthy, so I made the choice to add more green vegetables to my diet. The first few weeks were brutal. Green peppers in particular—the thought of eating one would give me chills. But I chose to eat green peppers several times a week—cooked and raw—because I had a goal to achieve.

A month or so into adding more green vegetables into my diet, I realized I actually began to like them—even those green peppers. Years ago, I tended to stay away from green vegetables. Now, after making the right choice over and over—even when I didn't want to, even when it was hard—I changed my natural tendency. Now, I tend to crave green vegetables and look forward to meals with more of them in it. I *tend* to take action to lead me closer to who and where I want to be.

Enough with the food talk! If you're looking to be more successful, to live out your purpose, to achieve the goals set within your heart, I want you to succeed. Success doesn't happen overnight; it happens over time. What you do today will affect where you are tomorrow. Keep your head up. Put in the hard work to make better choices. It's in your choices that you'll shift your tendencies…you'll become the person who *tends* to succeed at everything they do!

Ideas to Accelerate My Success

_____

_____

_____

_____

_____

_____

_____

_____

CHAPTER 3

The Key to Confidence

"Yesterday's successes provide the confidence you need for today's challenges." —PHILLIP VAN HOOSER

Do you know someone—a family member, friend, business owner, team member, associate—who has failed to reach full professional potential for no other apparent reason than that they lacked confidence in themselves and their abilities?

If so, it's sad to witness, isn't it?

While you're thinking about it, let me ask an even more personal question: Does this possibly describe you? Have you ever struggled with the personal confidence needed to succeed? Do you lack the self-assurance to try something new or different? If so, how does it make you feel? Is it a pleasant, rewarding experience? Probably not.

Lack of confidence is an unfortunate malady affecting far too many business professionals. It's an obstacle to success that needs to be identified, addressed, and overcome. So, let's address the concept of confidence: how to get it, how to use it, and how to keep it.

To tackle this problem, you must first realize only one thing will build confidence in any human being. But before I share the one thing, let's look at three things some people think will make them more confident—but won't.

1. Confidence is not established by education alone. Intense study yielding advanced degrees will certainly help broaden your understanding of a specific subject area. But education alone will not sufficiently build your level of confidence.

2. Confidence is not built by effort alone. We all know many industrious people who work long and hard but continue to be unsuccessful in developing higher levels of personal confidence.

3. Finally, confidence is not established by repetition alone. Doing something repeatedly may create a personal comfort level forged in familiarity. But repetition of one task won't necessarily transfer confidence to new and different tasks.

So then, if education, effort, and repetition are not the magic potions guaranteed to build personal confidence, what is? What is the one thing that will allow you to soar confidently while others quake in their boots?

That one thing is…success! Simple, garden-variety success.

> "Success breeds success!"

Think about it. With every acknowledged success in life—be it large or small—our confidence in our abilities and our potential soars, even if only momentarily. While basking in the afterglow of a personal success, our confidence levels will naturally be at their highest peak.

It is in those special moments that our mind expands. This is when we're most open to new opportunities—chances to try new things. So, to intentionally prolong these heightened levels of confidence, we must consciously focus on the successes that got us where we are.

How do you do that? Try this activity.

Make a list of all your noteworthy accomplishments. No success is too large—or small—to be captured. Include past successes from grade school, high school, and college. Don't overlook your successful experiences in sports, volunteer, or extracurricular activities. And, of course, capture every success imaginable from your past work experiences, including those involving projects, people, and promotions.

Once you've developed your comprehensive list of successes, it's time to note what you've learned or gained from each. Ask yourself questions like:

- What new talent did I discover?
- What new skill was I able to learn or develop?
- What relationship was I able to grow?

Finally, ask yourself honestly if you're currently using all these tools at your disposal. If not, why not?

You can be confident of this—yesterday's successes provide the confidence you need for today's challenges, which in turn becomes the springboard for your future growth. Success breeds success!

Ideas to Accelerate My Success

CATALYST 2

Planning

CHAPTER 4

Planning to Plan

"We don't have to 'wait and see'—we can plan and 'work.'" —PHILLIP VAN HOOSER

At least once a year, our creative team carves out dedicated time for focused planning. As a group, we sit down, huddle together, and begin mentally sculpting our professional objectives, plans, and activities for the months ahead. Sometimes we invest a few hours in the activity; sometimes it's a few days. The commitment of time is relative to the scope and complexity of what we're planning.

But one thing is always certain: we're going to make time for planning. Why? Because over the years, our planning exercises have proven to be both a productive and profitable use of our time and collective brainpower. Personally, I'm totally committed to planning. I believe planning is a huge success accelerant!

But there are still many who don't share the same enthusiasm for, or commitment to, the act of planning. Some business professionals, entrepreneurs, and owners never seem to find the time or the inclination to create formal plans for their success strategy.

These folks are easy to spot. They're the ones making comments like, "We'll just have to wait and see..." or "Time will tell..." or "We'll cross that bridge when we get there."

In my humble opinion, such statements are essentially comfortable cop-outs. The fact is, we don't have to "wait and see"—we can "plan and work." "Time WILL tell!" It will tell if we have planned well and executed our plans. And yes, there are bridges to be crossed along our personal and professional journeys. However, successful professionals have learned to plan their chosen routes carefully, anticipating and avoiding as many obstacles as possible.

So, if you want to be more successful, be a better planner. Here are a few ideas to help you get started.

1. Identify specifically what you're planning. Organizations plan for productivity and profitability, personnel development and performance, even corporate and social responsibility. They have to. In a very real sense, their future depends on the plans they make. But what about individual team leaders, associates, and business professionals? What about you?

At the very least, you should formulate plans for your own physical health and fitness, your financial security, your professional marketability, as well as your emotional balance and spiritual significance. There is plenty to be planned. Be sure you know what you're working toward.

2. Establish a crystal-clear planning perspective. Rome wasn't built in a day. And there's no reason to think you can complete and fulfill all your plans in a day, a week, a month, or even a year. The key is to have a clear perspective. Perspective begins by knowing who is responsible for what and what the performance expectations are.

Here's a word to the wise: strive for sustainable excellence, not unattainable perfection in the completion of the plans you make.

3. Finally, establish a system for tracking your performance progress. Planning should not be an end unto itself. The plans you make should culminate in some sort of actual performance improvement. The real value lies in always tracking the performance improvements you've so carefully planned for.

Time management gurus have conservatively estimated that for every unit of time spent planning, four or more units of time can be saved in actual plan implementation and performance. In other words, if you spend an hour, a week, or a month planning an activity, you can reasonably expect to save four or more hours, weeks, or months once the activity is undertaken. For me, that's a great return on investment! One worth the plans I will commit to make in the days ahead. How's that for a plan?

Ideas to Accelerate My Success

_____

_____

CHAPTER 5

Blind Spots in Your Planning

"Without connecting the decision-makers and the frontline workers, decisions get made without all the information." —ALYSON VAN HOOSER

Unlike some, I've experienced working on the front lines and sitting at the board table—at the same time. This was incredibly eye-opening. Year after year, I saw blind spots, or disconnects, between what owners and decision-makers thought was happening and what was really going on day to day. Some blind spots weren't worth dissecting. Others changed the course of the organization's direction and success.

Without connecting the decision-makers and the frontline workers, decisions get made without all the information. That's like putting on shorts because it's sunny, but then walking outside to discover it's only 37 degrees. You can't make the *best* decision without *all* the information. Use this tip to help uncover information hiding in plain sight.

Step One in the Strategic Planning Process

You've gathered your team to take on the strategic planning process. It likely consists of team members and decision-makers from all departments, right?

The first step in the strategic planning process is typically centered around your vision statement, mission statement, and ultimately figuring out who and where you are right now. So each team leader has read the reports, analyzed the audits, and formed conclusions about where you are. They're ready to knock out step one!

Gathering that team and analyzing the formal data is a smart move to make. However, if that's the *only* move you make, you're asking for blind spots and disconnects. You have to uncover those! If you don't, you'll likely end up with a strategic plan that fails.

Dig Deeper Than the Numbers

Many leaders invest a huge amount of time digging into reports. Dig deeper than what's found in reports by internal and external auditors. They don't always contain all the answers or information. They're needed, but you need more than that if you're going to level up your planning. Start involving frontline team members, or at least frontline supervisors. Whether you want to believe it or not, their experience—even if it's limited—can uncover information a report or audit never can. The reports may show that your organization is performing, but if you're out of touch with your frontline people, you may miss that they see and feel a completely different story.

Getting Your People to Open Up

Here's a process you can use to help break down barriers between decision-makers and associates in order to uncover the information you need. Added benefit: most associates will LOVE you for including them and valuing their input!

1. Explain the strategic planning process to team members. If someone has never served as a decision-maker, they may have no idea what strategic planning even means. Help them understand what you're working on before you start trying to get information from them.

2. Communicate to them that you need all the information in order to make the best decision for them and for the company. Show them how important they are to making this happen.

3. Discuss your vision statement, mission statement, values—whatever it is you use to define your organization. Talk about it with team members, and ask them if they think this is an accurate picture of daily life within the organization.

4. Show and explain to them the audits and reports you have processed up to this point. Make sure you do this in a way they can understand. They may not have the same experience or education to understand them as quickly or as well as you do. On the other hand, if you try to make it too simple for someone who is already knowledgeable enough to understand, you may hurt their feelings.

5. Ask them where you're wrong. This may be hard for you, but people appreciate a humble decision-maker. Listen carefully as you let them talk. Take notes. Learn.

6. Once the strategic planning process is finished, follow up with the team members you involved. They'll be wondering about the outcome because they've now played a part in it. Don't leave them hanging. Nobody likes that.

Successful Step One

Decision-makers need all the information to make the best decisions…not some of the information, not the information they want to believe, not the information that is easy to gather—but *all* the information. When you gather more information directly from your team members, you're giving yourself a better chance at successfully creating and implementing your strategic plan.

Ideas to Accelerate My Success

CHAPTER 6

Invest Early, Invest Often

"If you invest early and often in your professional development, what you learn today will compound significantly over the course of your life and career." —PHILLIP VAN HOOSER

Let's begin with a simple scenario. A young professional asks your best advice for their life and career. So, what do you say? Have you taken time to think about it? If not, don't worry; we're about to.

I don't know if it's because my hair has started turning white—and turning loose—or if it's because my children have begun careers of their own. But more and more, I'm being asked, "Phil, what's your best advice for my life and career?"

And here's what I say:

"Invest early, and invest often."

Here's why.

Warren Buffet, longtime chairman and CEO of investment firm Berkshire Hathaway and arguably the most successful investor of all time, once explained his phenomenal success this way: "My wealth," he said, "has come from a combination of living in America, some lucky genes, and compound interest."

Like Buffet, I recognize the benefit of living in America—a democracy built on free enterprise—where dreams can and do still come true.

Like Buffet, most of us enjoy genes consistent with moderate longevity, allowing us a lifetime for opportunities and investment growth.

But unfortunately, unlike Buffet, I fear too many business professionals ignore and, therefore, forfeit a phenomenal tool hidden in plain sight. And that is the often underappreciated opportunity known as compound interest.

From a strictly financial perspective, consider the foundational difference between simple and compound interest. Simple interest applies to the original principal alone, whereas compound interest is earned not only on the original principal, but on the original principal plus all the other interest earned previously.

Here's an example of simple interest at work:

You invest $1,000 at 10 percent per year. And at the end of the Year 1, you will have earned $100 in interest.

Then in Year 2, simple interest is again applied, but only to your original $1,000 principal. At a 10 percent interest rate, you earn another $100 interest for the year. So at the end of two years, you will have your $1,000 principal and $200 in simple interest earned.

Now compare the same example using compound interest. You invest $1,000 at 10 percent per year. And at the end of the Year 1, you've earned $100 in interest—exactly the same as in our simple interest example.

But with the benefit of compound interest, you now begin Year 2 with a $1,100 investment—your original $1000 principal, plus the $100 interest earned from Year 1. And with a 10 percent annual interest rate, Year 2 will yield $110 in compound interest earned. At the end of two years, as a result of compound interest, you will have 5 percent more than you would have earned by simple interest.

I encourage you to do the math. A side-by-side comparison of simple versus compound interest over an extended period quickly reveals that even with modest annual gains, the long-term result can be astonishing. It's easy to understand why Albert Einstein referred to compound interest as the "eighth wonder of the world."

By the way, this same principal applies to "compounding professionalism." If you invest rationally and intentionally, early and often, in your own professional development, what you learn today has the opportunity to compound significantly over the course of your life and career.

At the same time, investing in the professional development of others yields compounding opportunities that can provide even more momentum.

So the next time you're seeking advice, don't forget the financial and professional compounding effects of investing early and investing often.

Ideas to Accelerate My Success

_____

_____

_____

_____

_____

_____

_____

_____

_____

_____

_____

_____

_____

_____

_____

_____

_____

_____

_____

_____

_____

_____

_____

_____

_____

CATALYST 3

Communicating

CHAPTER 7

The Look

"When you don't give the best of your attention, you don't get the best of their information." —PHILLIP VAN HOOSER

You're exiting a meeting when you encounter a team member waiting patiently for you in the hallway. The person steps forward and poses a simple question.

"Excuse me, but may I talk with you for a moment?"

Of course your answer is likely to be "yes." Even the most unprofessional businessperson wouldn't blurt out: "No, I don't have time to talk with you. I'm far too busy for an unplanned conversation right now."

So, you say "yes." But unfortunately, your "yes" too often proves to be a "qualified" yes. As in, "Yes, of course you can talk with me," before adding thoughtlessly, "just walk with me as we talk. I've got someplace important I really need to be."

Guess what? You may not like to hear this, but you just blew it.

"Blew what? I said 'yes.' What else am I supposed to do?"

For starters, you should stop, look, and listen.

It happens regularly in organizations around the globe. Would-be professionals rush from Point A to Point B, desperately trying to multitask their way to success and significance. There will always be people to see, places to go, things to do. After all, that's how "important people" act, right?

Maybe so. But that's not how business *professionals* act. Real pros—the best ones—are famous for making time for team members, associates, colleagues, and others contributors. And by doing so, they make people feel special.

Let me sound a cautionary note right here. The technique I'm about to share may seem a bit simplistic to some. They may even be tempted to blow this whole idea off as unworthy of careful consideration and implementation.

Please don't be fooled. Business owners, entrepreneurs, and team leaders need unfettered communication with team members in the same way a vehicle needs fuel. The engine of business progress simply won't turn without it.

Not pausing long enough to look directly at someone speaking to you gives unmistakable evidence of this: whatever they have to say is far less important to you than whatever you're already heading toward.

Once that is understood, the original message the person was attempting to communicate to you changes. Sometimes, it gets shorter—out of necessity. Sometimes it gets harsher—out of frustration. Sometimes it gets withheld completely—out of spite.

Regardless, you can be sure that you're not getting the best of their information, because you're not giving the best of your attention.

So, the next time someone asks to speak with you, try this. Try to consciously—intentionally—stop what you're doing and turn your full attention to the person in question. Look at them. I mean it—look right at them. And while looking, listen carefully to what they have to say.

You may see more clearly the quality and importance of what they have to say. After all, it's not unusual to find the answers to our most perplexing business questions hidden in plain sight. You just have to be willing to look.

Ideas to Accelerate My Success

_____

_____

_____

_____

_____

_____

_____

_____

_____

_____

_____

_____

CHAPTER 8

Talking about People... Always a Bad Idea?

*"Communication is not just the words you speak...
it's why, how, when, what, and where you
interact with someone."* —ALYSON VAN HOOSER

As a business professional, you should talk *with* customers and team members. You should talk with them, not *to* them, and never *at* them. But should you talk *about* them? Well, it depends. Let's talk.

Picture it. As you approach a corner in the hallway, you hear your supervisor talking negatively about one of your co-workers. You think to yourself, *Surely this is a conversation with HR or with the co-worker's supervisor.* But you turn the corner to find your supervisor having a discussion about one of your co-workers with another one of your co-workers. After a quick peek, you turn around and head in the other direction. The entire walk back to your desk, your internal monologue oozes with thoughts of distrust, disrespect, and disgust for your supervisor.

Sadly, situations like these happen often. Society does—and has for centuries—held leaders to a higher standard. When you're a leader, you must hold yourself to that higher standard—you can bet your customers and associates do! Strong relationships are built on a foundation of trust. If your people can't trust you, they'll be questioning everything you say, confused by what you do, and unsure if they should support you. Ultimately, they may leave you.

To build and maintain trust with your people, here are the three ways you should approach talking about people.

Where: Publicly vs. Privately

Have you heard some version of the popular phrase "praise in public, punish in private"? This applies to anyone wanting to be respected and trusted. Know that it's great to brag about people publicly. Spread those words of praise in public like confetti on New Year's Eve all day, every day!

However, if it's negative, that's a conversation that should happen privately, behind closed doors, and with only that person. If it's work-related, then have that conversation only with your supervisor or HR.

If you don't handle the situation this way, people could begin questioning your character and decide not to have anything to do with you.

Who: Up, Not Down

This is the only time you will hear me put "leadership weight" in someone's position. Leadership in any organization is not about your position but rather your willingness to serve and take action. However, in this very specific situation, a person's position in the organization must be taken into account.

Think about your organizational chart. When it comes to an issue, talk up the chart, not down the chart. Your standard should be this: you will not discuss issues with anyone below you on the organizational chart—only above you.

Why shouldn't you discuss issues with the people below you on the chart? Instinctively, people believe they should be able to trust their leaders have their best interests at heart. They don't naturally feel the same way about their co-workers.

As a leader, you have to separate yourself from your team members. If you share confidential, potentially hurtful information with an associate's co-worker, you're opening the door for *all* of your associates to lose faith in you.

Additionally, you shouldn't be putting nails into your team's coffin. If you start talking bad about one team member to another, you're creating an environment where people start working against one another. Trust is broken between all of you, and that can be the demise of any good team.

When: Not at All

There are times when you should and should not discuss another person with someone else. If you're searching for a solution to a problem, seek guidance the right way.

If you're just wanting to vent about someone—don't. As a human being, there is no good reason to speak in any negative light about someone else simply because a short venting session might make you feel good. This is where emotional intelligence is key.

If you've let another person work you up and you don't actually need guidance on how to manage the situation, you're actually seeking an emotional release for yourself. When that's the case, find a healthy way to deal with it. Go for a walk. Eat a Snickers®. Take time away from the situation, and work on something else. Go back to deal with it when you're level-headed.

Communicate on Purpose

Communication is not just the words you speak…it's why, how, when, what, and where you interact with someone. Communication is a skill that can absolutely make or break your personal and professional success. Understanding if/when/ how to talk about people is a foundational expectation from anyone you're looking to impact, lead, or influence. Make sure you do it right.

Ideas to Accelerate My Success

_____

_____

_____

_____

_____

_____

_____

_____

_____

_____

_____

_____

_____

_____

_____

_____

_____

_____

_____

_____

_____

_____

_____

CHAPTER 9

I'm Sorry, and I Really Mean It

"Business professionals never look good by making others look bad." —PHILLIP VAN HOOSER

Several years ago, I stumbled across a troubling statistic. While I'm unable to name the original source and I cannot verify its accuracy, I've never been able to get this particular statistic out of my mind.

Here it is: Only 48 percent of the general population will offer an apology, even if an apology is thought to be appropriate and justified.

Let's say that a different way. A full 52 percent—more than half the general population—will not apologize, regardless of the level of appropriateness and justification.

Think for a minute. What would result if business owners, entrepreneurs, sales associates, and customer service professionals were surveyed?

Would a higher percentage of these professionals be willing to apologize for their mistakes when compared to the general population? Or would it be a lower percentage? What do you think?

You can easily guess what my hope would be. I would hope the percentage of appropriate, voluntary apologies coming from business professionals would be higher—much higher—than the general population. But honestly, I just don't know. And to me, that's sad.

In case you happen to be a professional who struggles with apologizing when necessary, I have something that can help. The wonderful book *Crucial Conversations: Tools for Talking When Stakes Are High* contains the following definition of an apology:

"An apology is a statement that sincerely expresses your sorrow for your role in causing—or at least not preventing—pain or difficulty to others."

That's a pretty good start. But to be adequately prepared to apologize once the need arises, I think even more is needed. Here's a four-step process for apologizing.

1. **Acknowledge the specific offense.** A word to the wise: don't be cute. Don't try to ignore, sidestep, or downplay the obvious. Look the situation square in the eye and call it what it is: a foolish mistake, an unnecessary oversight, or an unfortunate omission—whatever it is. But always be specific as to why you're apologizing.

2. **Offer a plausible explanation for what occurred, if appropriate.** Again, don't try to play games. To the best of your ability, offer a brief but factual account of what happened. And although it may be tempting to do so, don't throw others under the bus in an attempt to defend your own ill-advised words or actions. Remember, business professionals never look good by making others look bad.

3. **Offer a sincere expression of regret.** Stand up straight, look people in the eye, and let them see that you're accepting full responsibility for your actions. Let them know that you'll never let anything like this happen again. And don't be afraid to ask for forgiveness.

4. **Provide some sort of restitution.** Acknowledging the offense, offering an explanation for it, and expressing regret are all important steps when apologizing. But in the end, people want to know specifically what you're committed to doing to make things right—to make amends. Confession is good for the soul, but restitution is good for the relationship!

"If you mess up, you've got to fess up."

Saying "I'm sorry" seems to come easier for some than others. But for successful business professionals, there's no option. If you mess up, you've got to fess up. By apologizing the right way, both your words and your actions send the message, "I'm sorry, and I really mean it."

Ideas to Accelerate My Success

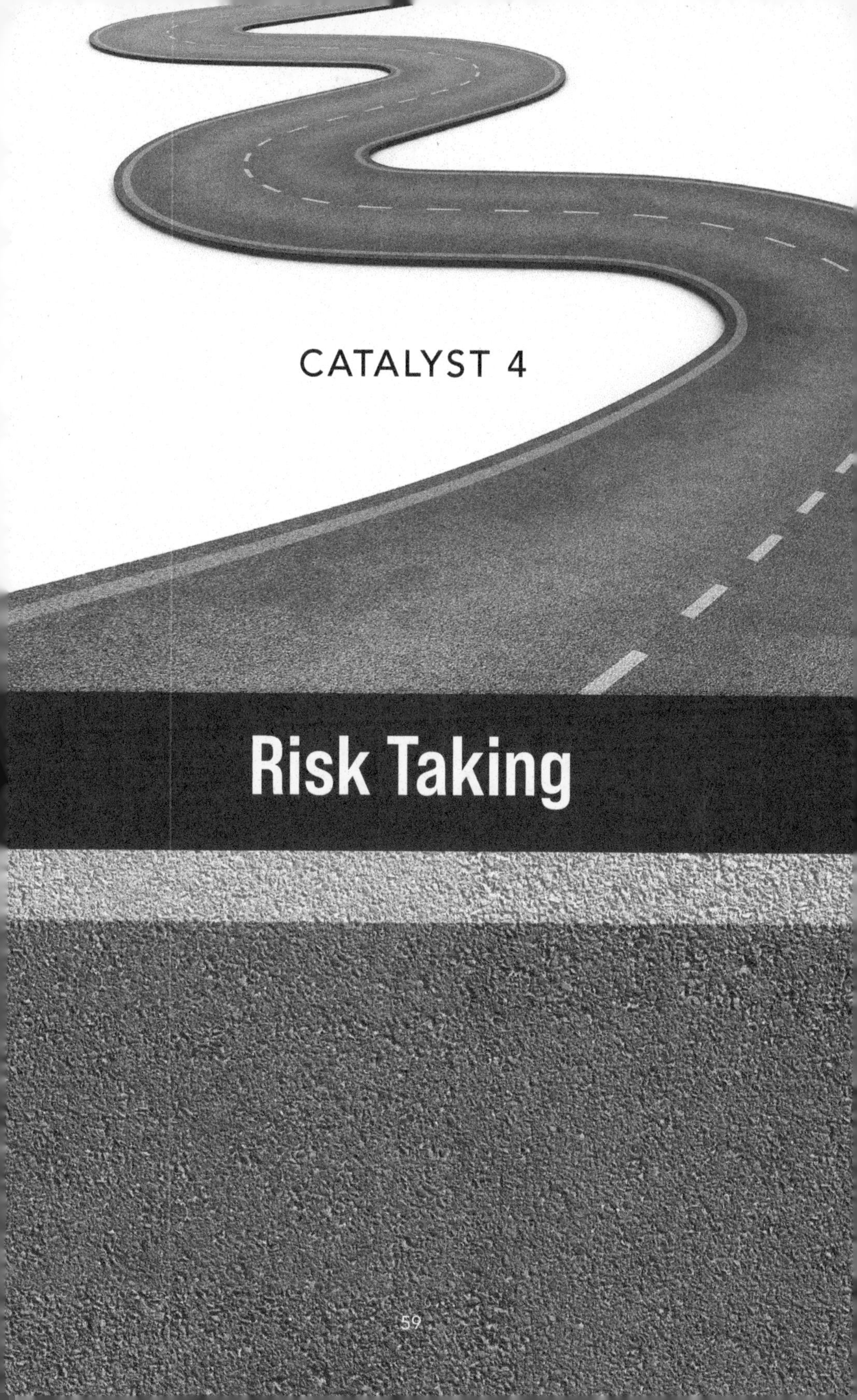

CATALYST 4

Risk Taking

Embrace Your Opportunity

"If you're willing to see yourself as successful and take the risks to make it happen, opportunities are certain to follow." —PHILLIP VAN HOOSER

I'm not much into hero worship, but I admit to having at least one. Hilary Hinton Ziglar, more commonly known as Zig Ziglar!

Zig Ziglar's no longer with us, but his powerful legacy lives on. I knew Zig as a professional colleague, and I knew him to be the real deal—every bit as positive and encouraging one on one as when he was one on one thousand.

I once overheard a conversation between Zig and another professional speaking colleague of ours. This gentleman was attempting to justify his complacency in a particular matter by claiming limitations imposed by his current situation. Zig wasn't buying it.

"I couldn't possibly do that," the young man argued, "I'm just a…" He made it no further.

"Friend," Zig interrupted, "just because a momma cat has her kittens in the oven—that don't make 'em biscuits!"

Confused? It may take you a minute or two to process that one, so let me help.

Homespun as it may have been, Zig's statement was intended to encourage the young man to look beyond where he was, what he was doing, and how he perceived his present situation. He was challenging him to look toward what he ultimately *could be* and *do*.

You may be wondering if striving for success is for you. In fact, you may be thinking, "I'm just a…" Go ahead, fill in the blank.

Do you see yourself as JUST a team member, JUST a service associate, JUST a mechanic, JUST an accountant, JUST an engineer, JUST a salesperson, JUST a mother, JUST a father, JUST an anything?

If so, I'm here to tell you, you're already selling yourself short. Others—your boss, your peers, your neighbors, your family—treat you as they *see you seeing yourself.*

Ultimately, success is not based on your position. So, no one else limits your potential to succeed. That's on you. If you're willing to see yourself as successful and take the risks to make it happen, opportunities are certain to follow.

This book is a tool to help you build a strong foundation for professional success. But the process begins by making a personal commitment to embracing your current position and exercising the opportunities available to you right now.

Remember Zig's "kittens and biscuits" analogy? I'll suggest one of the first lessons of professional success is this: no one cares where you started or where you've been. Your professional history is simply not of concern to them. Instead, what is of greatest concern to others is what you are willing to do for them right now, right where you are.

For example, begin proving your professional worth today by going out of your way to acknowledge and congratulate someone on a recent job well done, or by going out of your way to support and encourage someone who has experienced some recent difficulty or disappointment. When you take intentional actions to serve and support others, your journey to professional success will be underway!

Ideas to Accelerate My Success

_____

_____

_____

_____

_____

_____

_____

_____

_____

_____

CHAPTER 11

Ask for Opportunity

"YOU control your success... Will you be bold enough to ask for it?" —ALYSON VAN HOOSER

There is enough opportunity out there for all of us—ALL OF US! But for you to get it, you have to be willing to do what it takes. Sometimes all it takes for you to get opportunity is to be bold enough to step up and ask for it. Let's dig into how having the courage to ask for opportunity worked for me and how it can work for you, too!

I had been in my management role a little over a year when the CEO asked all the managers to complete a succession plan. If you aren't familiar with succession planning, it basically answers this question: Who will take my place when I get promoted, quit, or am no longer able to do my job?

As I started digging into the analytics, my thoughts about my department were confirmed. Customer traffic was down. Managers across our team had the bandwidth to manage more people. There were also multiple projects we should be working on that would add to our profits. What did all of this mean? Bottom line—it meant the research showed there was no need for my current position.

I was a new employee, a young employee. This was my first big project at this company, and all the research I had done came down to *this?!* I did not want to present my succession plan and say, "You should fire me." I had to have a job!

So, I figured out a way to make this a win-win for everyone. I started detailing the organizational weaknesses and aligning them with my strengths. There were problems I could fix. There were value strategies and projects I could implement and manage that would add to our growth! This was my opportunity, but was I bold enough to ask for it?

No Need for My Position

When the time came, I stood in the board room before senior management and gave them what they asked for—a personal recommendation for who could effectively fill my current position and why. They were all pleased.

But then I turned my presentation from tradition to innovation. And some of their faces went from smiles of support to absolute shock!

I thoroughly explained to them how the business numbers proved there was no longer a need for my current position within the company. The only reason to keep me in that current role would be because "that's the way we've always done it." And that way was not helping the business.

Boldly Ask

I went on to explore important unmet needs within the company and share my idea for how a new position could fix them. They saw the needs, and they agreed.

Then I stepped up to the plate and asked for the opportunity. I was sweating bullets and my heart was racing, but I gave them every reason why I was the best fit for this new position. I closed the presentation by asking for the opportunity to fill this new position.

The room was silent. I left that meeting without direction or feedback. It was brutal. However, executive management finished out the fiscal year by eliminating my current position and creating a new, more strategic, more profitable position within the company.

Who got the new job? That's right—I did!

Where Could You Be

I sought out opportunity when it looked like there was none—and I asked for it. I have no doubt I got the opportunity because I mustered up enough courage to boldly ask for it.

You can get what you want, but you have to ask for it. Where could you be if you sought out opportunity and then took the bold steps to ask for it?

YOU control your success. The question is: Will you be bold enough to ask for it?

Ideas to Accelerate My Success

CHAPTER 12

In Over Your Head

"What you do is far less important than the attitude
that drives what you do." —PHILLIP VAN HOOSER

During a canoeing adventure on Missouri's scenic Current River, a relaxing day with my friends quickly changed. A bend in the river revealed a concentration of abandoned canoes, their former occupants swinging merrily—one by one—from a rope attached to a large tree limb jutting out over the river.

As an observer, it looked like great fun! As a participant, I wanted no part of it. Why? Not because of the rope, the height, or even the ultimate plunge into the cold water. Simply put, I lacked confidence in my swimming skills. And lacking confidence, I was sorely tempted to embrace complacency—and stay in my boat.

My friends decided to participate, and they dared me to do the same. Finally, I could resist the pressure no longer. With my adrenalin pumping and my heart beating wildly, I grasped the rope and launched myself forward out over the river pool below. Companions and strangers alike joined in a chorus of encouragement. But after releasing the rope and tumbling into the chilly waters, I was alone.

And I was in over my head.

The river's gentle current quickly began pulling me downstream, away from my friends. Panicking, I kicked and flailed. And as a result, I tired quickly. Soon I had no other option—I had to pause and rest.

When I did, I made a significant discovery. I was no longer in over my head. The water in which I'd initially struggled was now less than waist deep. Sheepishly, hoping no one else saw this revelation, I waded back to my canoe.

This over-my-head river experience reminds me of an important question for business professionals pursuing greater success. T.S. Eliot is believed to have asked, "If you're not in over your head, how do you know how tall you are?"

It's a tragic fact that some professionals choose personal comfort by embracing complacency. And because of a complacent attitude, many problems arise. You see, personal comfort often leads to personal inaction. We choose not to do anything, or at least nothing new. And inactivity—be it mental or physical—inevitably leads to decreased and deteriorating performance. And as our performance deteriorates, so does our ability to positively influence and impact others.

So, here's a simple challenge intended to counteract complacency. And as my canoeing friends did with me, I'll do for you—I'll dare you to take the challenge.

First, for fun, I dare you to go to some new, exotic restaurant and order the Chef's Surprise. Don't look at the menu. Don't ask the waiter for a description of what you'll get. Don't even ask the price. Just take the leap! It will be fun—I promise!

Then on a professional level, I dare you to ask your team leader for more responsibility. Seriously!

For example, ask to be assigned to an internal performance improvement team. Or ask permission to revise your company's new hire onboarding and orientation process. Or volunteer to teach some skill you possess to those interested in knowing what you already know.

In other words, get out of your comfortable boat and swing into action. You'll be better for the experience—I promise!

This is the key to remember: what you do is far less important than the attitude that drives what you do.

Yes, I know your work plate is full. I also know it's easy to get too comfortable in that safe little boat of yours. There's no better time than the present to take the plunge. I bet the water in which you land will be manageable. I expect the experience will prove invigorating. And I imagine, if you actually get in over your head, it won't be long at all until you're standing tall again!

Ideas to Accelerate My Success

_____

_____

_____

_____

CATALYST 5

Performance

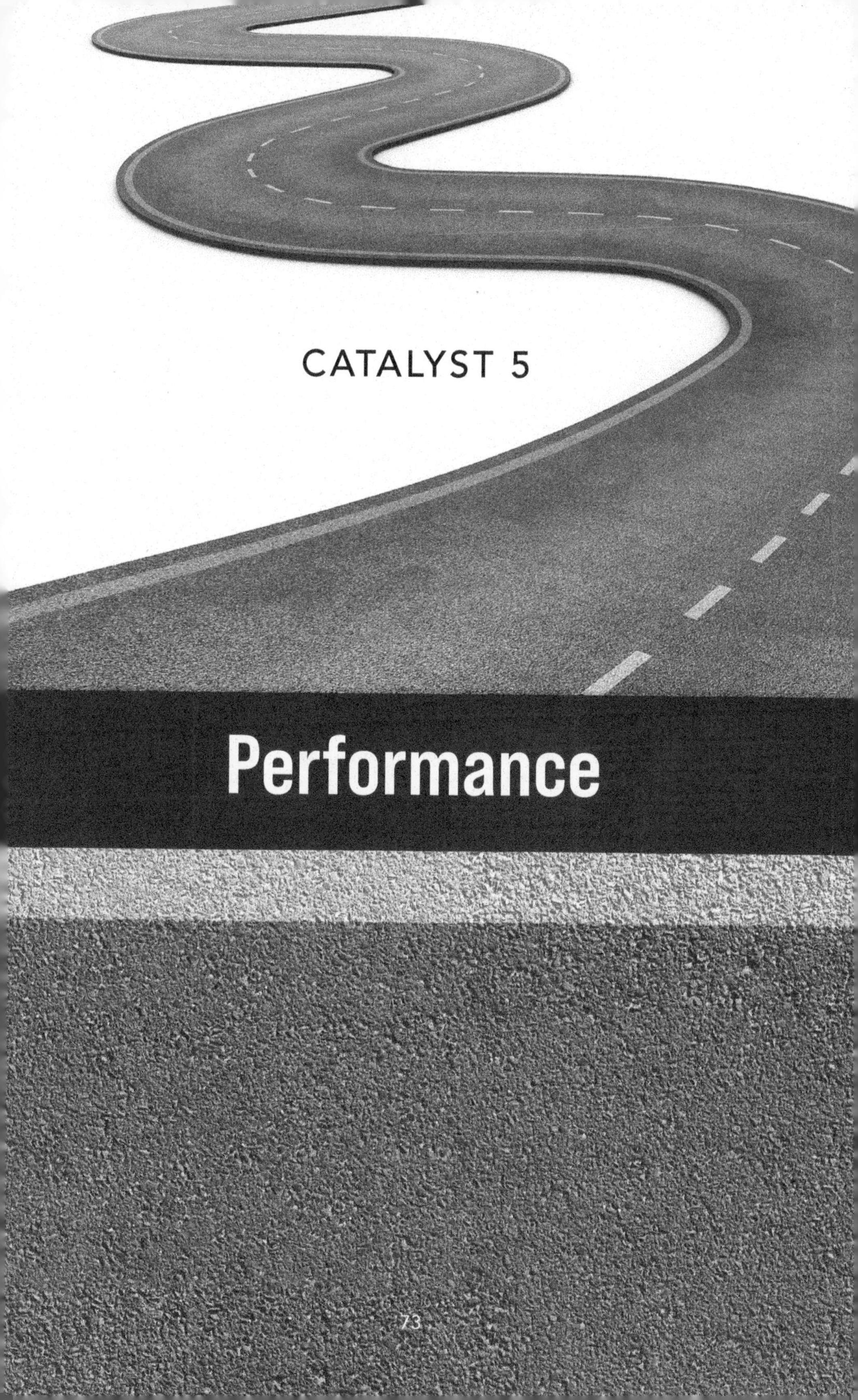

CHAPTER 13

The 3 Cs of Results-Driven Action

"Desire alone will not get you closer to crushing your goals. You have to take action." —ALYSON VAN HOOSER

Do you really want to be more successful? Understanding the right action you need to take is critical for earning success. Without a high-level understanding of what you *do* and *do not* need to do, you'll be left with long-term, lackluster results.

In my book, *LEVEL UP: Elevate Your Game & Crush Your Goals,* I open by laying the foundation with three Cs. The three Cs for results-driven action will help you take control of your future success and eliminate wasted time and energy!

C #1: Correct

The first of the three Cs is CORRECT. You must take correct action. Anything else will get you off track from accomplishing your goals.

I suggest the first step in establishing what correct action looks like for you is to get your perspective in check. Understanding who you are, what you want to achieve, and how the world *really* works is key to correctly seeing what action you need to take.

How do you know if your perspective is currently correct or incorrect? Answer this question for yourself: When is the last time I sat down and deeply analyzed who I am, my goals, and the world around me?

- If your answer is never, you could be taking incorrect action.

- If your answer is sometime before your mid-20s, you could be taking incorrect action. Why? The decision-making part of your brain isn't fully developed until you're in your mid-20s.

- If your answer is six months ago, then you may very well be on the right track!

Hear me carefully: correct, results-driven action is critical to building the right foundation for you to grow from.

C #2: Calculated

Calculated action means every action you take is on purpose, for a purpose. In other words, every word you say and every move you make is to get you closer to—not further from—crushing your goals.

How do you learn what action to take and when? You must deeply understand the people around you.

Newsflash: There is no one in the world who is a self-made success. If you want to be successful, you're going to have to be willing to learn about and work well with other people. You must develop your knowledge of who the people are around you, what they like and dislike, what motivates them, what their goals are, and how they prefer to collaborate.

Why do you need to do this?

People are forming opinions about you with every interaction you have with them. Their opinion of you matters—it determines how they treat you. They may be your door to opportunity! Make sure you're interacting with them intentionally. And here's the thing: their opinion of you will have less to do with you and more to do with them.

- How do you make them feel?
- Do you cause them to have more or less faith in you?
- Do your actions make them want to invest in or avoid you?

That list could go on. People have different personalities and motivations. You need to understand them so you can adapt your actions and create forward progress in your personal and professional life.

C #3: Consistent

I believe your success hinges on your willingness to be consistent. Consistent action may be the hardest part of all of this.

Most people are not where they want to be in life because they don't consistently perform well.

The key to being consistent is to stay focused on your goals. When you clearly know what you are trying to accomplish, you're less likely to succumb to incorrect, uncalculated, inconsistent actions in the heat of the moment. Instead, you'll be more likely to choose the right actions, the right response, and the right decision.

My question to you is: Do you know *exactly* where you're headed? Do you have a *clear* goal? If not, you'll be taking a lot of action leading you nowhere.

I challenge you to get serious about naming and understanding your own priorities so when the rubber meets the road, you won't lose your motivation or your consistency.

Results-Driven Action for Success

The bottom line is this: you can have that hunger, that burning desire, or that small voice impelling you to live your value. But that feeling alone will not get you any closer to crushing your goals. You have to take action. And by action, I mean correct, calculated, and consistent action—right now. That is your only option for success.

Ideas to Accelerate My Success

_____

_____

_____

_____

_____

_____

_____

_____

_____

_____

_____

_____

_____

_____

_____

_____

_____

_____

_____

_____

_____

_____

_____

_____

_____

_____

_____

_____

_____

_____

_____

CHAPTER 14

Peak Performer Secrets 1 & 2

"We best control our thoughts when we direct them toward a concrete goal or action." —PHILLIP VAN HOOSER

Almost every day for the past 30-odd years, I've been blessed to interact with one high-performing individual after another. Some have been well-known public figures—business titans, bestselling authors, professional athletes, and successful entrepreneurs.

But far more of these high performers are virtually anonymous. They work their magic without fanfare or media buzz. Business professionals, managers, team members, sales and service associates, teachers, coaches, parents—people primarily recognized by those whose lives they touch. And over the years, these peak performers have taught me a few secrets you'll want to know.

Peak Performer Secret 1: Strong Desire to Exceed

Virtually every high performer I know has a strong desire to exceed. While the high performers around us may desire to exceed, underperformers seem satisfied to simply "relive." Many underperformers live in the past, clinging tightly to fleeting memories of former success and glory: tasks they accomplished, awards they received, promotions earned. All great of course, but all in the past.

Underperforming does not make someone a bad person, but it does result in wasted time, lost opportunities, and worse still—squandered talent. While peak performers may enjoy an occasional trip down memory lane, they don't pitch their tents and stake a claim there. There's simply no time. They are far too busy making new plans to realize new successes.

Take a minute and do a self-assessment of your performance level by answering these questions:

1. As a general rule, do you tend to look backward longingly at your accomplishments, or do you look forward expectantly to new goals?

2. For the challenges you face, do you tend to depend exclusively on your former knowledge, skills, and understanding—how you did it before? Or are you diligently studying, exploring, and developing appropriate strategies for the new challenges that are arising? Is your approach characterized by the old adage "If the

only tool you have is a hammer, every problem looks like a nail"?

3. Do you tend to ignore or resist a message like this one, thinking it's meant for someone else? Or does it start you thinking about the multitude of opportunities around you?

Peak Performer Secret 2: Crystallize Thinking into Goals

I grew up in rural western Kentucky, where I learned one of the most valuable performance lessons of my life: *If you don't know where you're going, any road will take you there. But you won't know when you get there because you never intended to be there in the first place.*

You see, being crystal clear about your destination is absolutely critical for long-term success in any venture. If we lack a clear vision, we're easily distracted and have no ultimate destination.

How many times have I heard people lament a lack of time to read, study, explore, or improve? Yet they can recite minute details of the previous evening's ballgame, sitcom, or some nonsensical facts discovered on the Internet.

Did I just step on your toes? If so, let me follow with this question: Who's really controlling your time and what you think about? I don't mean to be judgmental, but it's not you. We best control our thoughts when we direct them toward a concrete goal or action.

I don't presume to know your thoughts or goals, but since you're reading this, I'm going to assume you have a desire to be more successful. So, I'll suggest some things for you to think about, along with some possible goals for you to consider.

1. Think about what you're reading and its ultimate effect—if any—on your professional readiness. A personal goal, for example, might be to read at least 20 minutes daily. Simple enough. You choose the information source: newspaper or magazine articles, blogs, professional development podcasts, books like this one—whatever.

2. Think about whom you're interacting with and what you're learning from them. A personal goal might be to have lunch or a short telephone conversation monthly with a professional you admire and can learn from. Reach out to them. You may be amazed at their accessibility and willingness to share.

3. Think about the last time you spent time just thinking. A personal goal might be to treat yourself to a one-day retreat each year—at the beach, on the farm, or in your study. It's not the location; it's the isolation and solitude that count. Think about who you are as a professional, what you've accomplished, and how much farther you want to go.

In Lewis Carroll's famous book *Alice's Adventures in Wonderland*, there's a pivotal exchange between Alice and the Cheshire Cat.

"Would you tell me, please, which way I ought to go from here?"

"That depends a great deal on where you want to get to," said the Cat.

"I don't much care where—" said Alice.

"Then it doesn't matter which way you go," said the Cat.

When you crystallize your thinking into goals and maintain a strong desire to exceed, you'll be on the road to peak performance!

But there are two more peak performance secrets—keep reading!

Ideas to Accelerate My Success

_____

_____

_____

_____

_____

_____

_____

_____

_____

_____

_____

_____

CHAPTER 15

Peak Performer Secrets 3 & 4

"Education, experience, and growth reside in risky, uncomfortable, and stress-producing situations." —PHILLIP VAN HOOSER

Do you like sushi? Some people do; some people don't, and some people honestly don't know if they do. They've never tried it, and frankly, they have no intention of doing so!

You may be wondering, *What does sushi have to do with peak performance?* The peak performers I know share the common habit of getting outside their comfort zones.

Peak Performer Secret 3: Avoid the Comfort Zone

Our comfort zones may seem secure and stress-free, but in reality they hold us back. While most of us don't enjoy situations that are risky, uncomfortable, and stress-producing, that's where education, experience, and growth reside.

To reach greater levels of performance, we should expect, and even embrace, some degree of discomfort and uncertainty. Simply put: You have to try new things to learn new things—so that you can master new things. That's a fact.

But this is also a fact: those who desire safe, easy, stress-free professional comfort zones should prepare themselves for a career of repetition, tedium, complacency, monotony, and very little, if any, intellectual stimulation. For me, there's nothing comforting about that thought.

So, here's my challenge to you. It comes in the form of one of my personal peak performance philosophies: *if it scares me professionally, I'll try it—at least once.*

How can you be certain you can't do something if you don't try it? Can you really know you won't like something if you don't try it?

> "If it scares you professionally,
> try it—at least once."

The things I find most frightening generally are not the most dangerous. Instead, they are usually the most unfamiliar. Amazingly, once familiar, the fear, anxiety, and stress seem to evaporate almost like a mist. In its place comes the satisfaction of knowing I have grown and achieved something new.

I challenge you to step out of at least one of your comfort zones voluntarily—and into a growth zone. Volunteer for a task you've previously and intentionally avoided. Provide your team leader with a detailed suggestion—or possibly an implementation plan—to correct a nagging problem. Or contact someone you would like to learn from and invite him or her to lunch. And when you do, may I suggest the sushi!

Peak Performer Secret 4: Never Give Up

Each year since 1929, the Academy of Motion Picture Arts and Sciences has hosted what is commonly known as the Academy Awards. And each year since 1929, there's been much speculation, spirited debate, and general hoopla around which film will be named the year's Best Picture.

In 1968, the best picture was not *Cool Hand Luke*. But in my opinion, it should have been! *Cool Hand Luke* is probably my favorite movie of all time. It stars a young Paul Newman playing a nonconforming southern prison inmate. Want more plot? You'll have to rent it!

There's one scene involving a boxing match that won me over. In the scene, Luke is completely overmatched by a larger, stronger opponent, nicknamed Dragline. Dragline is administering Luke a savage beating, during which the following exchange occurs:

Dragline to Luke: "Stay down. You're beat."

Luke to Dragline (looking up from the ground, covered with mud and blood): "You're gonna hafta kill me." (And he struggled back to his feet.)

The world appreciates fighters—men and women who struggle to overcome apparently insurmountable odds on their way to becoming more than anyone ever imagined. This movie scene illustrates one more critical secret of peak performers. Peak performers never give up!

We will all encounter times when we must depend on our own internal resolve, times when we must buckle down, bow our necks, and do what is necessary—no matter how unpleasant—in order to get the job done.

Things don't always go exactly as you planned, and you can't just throw in the towel, quit, and go home. Your role as a business owner, entrepreneur, or business professional demands more. Those most important to you—those depending on you—expect more.

When you find yourself up against a wall, consider the perspective of this well-known peak performer. His early life was filled with multiple personal challenges. He struggled with serious asthma and other health issues as a child. As a young man, his wife and his beloved mother died on the same day. Shortly thereafter, he suffered tremendous financial loss. He led men into battle, and some died while under his command. And later in life, he even survived an assassin's bullet. In spite of, or possibly because of, these and other life challenges, Theodore Roosevelt became the youngest president of the United States, at that time, at the age of 43. Remember his words about peak performance:

"It is hard to fail, but it is worse never to have tried to succeed. Do what you can, with what you have, where you are. Far better it is to dare mighty things, to win glorious triumphs even though checkered by failure, than to rank with those poor spirits who

neither enjoy nor suffer much because they live in the gray twilight that knows neither victory nor defeat."

Ideas to Accelerate My Success

_____

_____

_____

_____

_____

_____

_____

_____

_____

_____

_____

_____

_____

_____

_____

_____

_____

_____

_____

_____

_____

_____

_____

_____

CATALYST 6

Emotional Intelligence

CHAPTER 16

The X Factor

"If you can control your emotions, you can control your performance, job satisfaction, and well-being." —ALYSON VAN HOOSER

If a team member asked for specific training to help them use the company intranet, understand the policies better, or improve their technical skills, you would probably do everything you could to get them the proper training to be successful, right?

What if there is training you could give them that they may not be bold enough to ask for or don't even recognize they need? And what if it's the X factor to elevate success for both of you? You would be all over that, wouldn't you?

What Is the X Factor

Many business owners, decision-makers, and leaders are quick to give opportunities if it will improve a team member's performance. Oftentimes those opportunities are focused on building *technical skills*. Improving technical skills is important to becoming more successful, but technical skills without soft skills will limit a person in what they can accomplish.

What's the most important soft skill? In my opinion—emotional intelligence. It's at the root of all we do. Developing emotional intelligence will check a lot of boxes for you and your people to become successful.

A Strategic Investment

At any given point in time, your associates may be handling a tough workload, preparing or giving high-pressure presentations, dealing with a difficult co-worker, celebrating a month-end success, or going through a rough season personally. The emotions generated by these experiences can affect our personal and/or professional lives. Those people who've developed the skill of controlling their emotions will ultimately be able to control their performance, job satisfaction, and well-being.

What Emotional Intelligence Is Not

Maybe you're rolling your eyes at the idea of investing time and resources into improving your emotional intelligence. Many people consider emotional intelligence to fall under the personal development umbrella. And when some people hear *personal development*, they picture some sort of therapy session, exercise program, snake oil advertisement, or a person named Wildflower who is going on sabbatical.

There are many reasons personal development training or practices have gotten a bad rap, but hear me out. You may be missing something—specifically, the impact of emotional intelligence on your business.

Hyperaware of Risks and Opportunities

The psychological term *emotional intelligence* means choosing to have "the capacity to be aware of, control, and express one's emotions, and to handle interpersonal relationships judiciously and empathetically."[1] In other words, becoming hyperaware of what is happening inside of you.

I use the word *hyperaware* intentionally. There is a difference between just being casually aware of something and being extremely or excessively aware of something. Those are two very different approaches. If you are casually aware of something, you might notice it every now and then. If you are hyperaware of something, then your antenna is constantly up. You are paying attention to every aspect of what is going on. So, when I say *hyperaware*, I mean being extremely aware of yourself internally and externally.

Catch & Crush

So how do you elevate your emotional intelligence instantly? You use my tried-and-true process: Catch & Crush. This method will help you process your feelings so that you can choose to either crush the feelings holding you back or use the feelings to help you crush your goals.

The next time you're in the midst of an emotionally elevated moment (e.g., participating in a big sales meeting, dealing with a disgruntled customer, putting on a swimsuit when you're 15 pounds heavier than where you want to be), think about what you're thinking. Yes, you read that right. Become hyperaware of the thoughts racing through your head. If you can write them down, do it. This is the CATCH part of the process. You're catching your initial thoughts and feelings as they're rising up inside you. What I know is that thoughts cause feelings and feelings can drive actions. In order to elevate your emotional intelligence, you must catch the thoughts racing through your head so that you can stop to evaluate the feeling they're causing and then decide what you need to do with them.

Step 1 is to stop and catch; step 2 is to CRUSH. Once you've caught what's going on inside you, now you have a choice to make: *Should I crush this feeling or use it to crush my goals?* It's as simple as that—a choice.

Let's say you have caught a thought and feeling that is holding you back. For example, maybe you're worried someone will ask you a question that you don't know the answer to and you're feeling insecure. That feeling isn't serving you well. So, if you know you're totally prepared, this might be a good time to crush the feeling. How do you do that on a practical level? Start by reciting logic over the irrational thought. You could literally think and say to yourself, "I am totally prepared for this moment." Say it over and over. Eventually, the insecurity might go away. But even if it doesn't in the moment, make sure you take action toward your goals regardless of your emotion. For this example, you don't ghost the person at the meeting—you show up and you show out. You're prepared, so make that known! That's how you crush feelings and still crush your goals!

On the other hand, you might have situations where thoughts and feelings can really help you crush your goals. For example, if you've been prepping for a triathlon and your last several training sessions went really well, you might be thinking you're going to kill this race and are feel really excited about the challenge. That's a feeling that can change how your body is operating physiologically. The adrenaline caused by that feeling can push you into a head start and pull you through when you hit a lull in your energy during the race. Hence, Catch & Crush to elevate your success.

Improve Your Performance

If you knew something was robbing you of your best success, wouldn't you take action to minimize the risk? Absolutely! Low emotional intelligence may be that risk. Developing your emotional intelligence is how you mitigate that risk. It's time to take action to improve your odds of success.

Ideas to Accelerate My Success

_____

_____

_____

_____

Note

1. "Emotional Intelligence," *Lexico*, Lexico.com, accessed June 7, 2021, https://www.lexico.com/en/definition/emotional_intelligence.

CHAPTER 17

I Don't Like That Man

"Do you do what you want to do or what you need to do as a professional?" —PHILLIP VAN HOOSER

I want you to think about three difficult questions and your answers for each. By the way, your professional reputation and success may very well rest in the answers you settle on.

Okay, here's Question 1: *Can you think of someone with whom you work or come into contact professionally whom you simply don't like?*

You know what I mean. Is there an individual who causes you to dread those occasions when you're forced to meet or interact? It could be a superior, a subordinate, a peer, a customer, a member, a vendor…the possibilities are virtually endless.

By the way, you've already answered the question if you're sitting there nodding and muttering a single name over and over.

So on to Question 2: *What specifically is it about this person you dislike?*

Can you put your finger on it? Are your feelings rooted in an attitude or a habit, or are they based on some past experience?

Now Question 3: *How do you normally treat this person?*

Practically speaking, this is the most important question of all. This is where the professional rubber meets the road.

Do you do what you *want* to do or what you *need* to do as a professional?

Truthfully, most of us *want* to avoid the people we dislike. But as a business owner, entrepreneur, team member, or any other kind of professional, we still *need* to be able to work with them.

Consciously separating ourselves from people—either physically or emotionally—can prove disastrous. Long-lasting damage can be done. And unfortunately, the existence of strained professional relationships can be an embarrassing testament to overall professional inadequacy.

So what can you do?

One of America's greatest leaders also happened to be one of the most hated men of his time. History records that Abraham Lincoln, as both man and president, was criticized, ridiculed, mocked, and second-guessed by friend and foe alike. If ever there was a person who could have justified the creation of an "enemies list," it was Honest Abe.

But Abraham Lincoln was a different kind of professional. And today, we can all learn from his example. Lincoln's greatness may be best illustrated by his own words. During a frank conversation with an associate regarding a political adversary, history records Lincoln as having stated bluntly, "I don't like that man."

But then, after a thoughtful pause, he added, "I think I need to get to know him better."

Powerful then? Without question! Possible now? Absolutely! But only when people intentionally choose to approach professional relationships—even the difficult ones—with the same honesty and emotional intelligence as practiced by Lincoln.

The long-term result? Well, your personal image may never be stamped on a penny, but your professional impact may forever leave its mark on those with whom you come in contact.

Ideas to Accelerate My Success

CHAPTER 18

Why People Act the Way They Do

"Understanding predictable responses gives us useful emotional intel to successfully defend and overcome the adversity." —PHILLIP VAN HOOSER

It's the one question I get asked most often in my leadership management training sessions. And it's fueled with bewilderment and exasperation. Here it is: *Why do people act the way they do?!*

The question reveals a real and serious frustration that business leaders, owners, entrepreneurs, and other professionals are experiencing. It is driven by their observations of what they consider misguided, irrational, or just plain nonsensical behaviors by otherwise rational, level-headed people.

The question indicates the significant need for people to strengthen and further develop their emotional intelligence. A lack of emotional intelligence is a major reason why we experience so much frustration and misunderstanding and why so much effort to motivate and inspire greater performance from other people falls flat.

All behavior—everything you do, I do, or anyone else does—is an attempt to consciously or subconsciously satisfy a need we have. I call it the "cornerstone concept." A really interesting thing happens when we apply that concept. We no longer have to ask "why" someone is acting as they are. We already have the answer to that question.

When we observe people acting in a rash, unpredictable manner, we can be reasonably sure they're responding to an unmet need. So the more important question we should be asking is "what?" What need is driving this behavior? This is an excellent opportunity for us to stretch our emotional intelligence muscles.

There are three common ways to find the answers to the "what" question. We can ask the person; we can ask others; or we can consistently observe the person's behavior. While some people may be willing to share their need, others may not realize what their need is or be willing to share it openly. Asking others may be the worst way to understand what is motivating a person's behavior. The information gained from others will always be colored by their own personal biases. But regularly observing a person's actions offers us the most consistent insight into the needs that are prompting their actions.

Life isn't perfect. We are on top one day, and the next day we feel like we're the central character in *Alexander and the*

Terrible, Horrible, No Good, Very Bad Day. This fact of life applies to everyone around us, too.

Knowing disappointment and difficulty can show up at any time should motivate us to prepare intellectually and emotionally in advance. Whether we are having a *no good, very bad day,* or it's one of our team members, a customer, or a close personal connection, understanding the predictable responses gives us useful emotional intel to successfully defend and overcome the adversity. Intuitively considering how people (ourselves included) behave in less-than-ideal circumstances expands our ability to minimize or prevent knee-jerk reactions.

These three behaviors may indicate someone has an unmet need.

1. Withdrawal

Withdrawal usually occurs in one of two ways: the most obvious way and the most common way. The most obvious form of withdrawal is physical withdrawal. People quit and leave. Team members, co-workers—even customers—leave because their needs aren't being satisfied. They go looking somewhere else for the satisfaction they need.

The other form of withdrawal is emotional withdrawal. We quit—but stay. We "check out," "disengage," "go through the motions," or "do just enough to get by." Our passion is waning, and our performance is wanting. It's not exactly a recipe for professionalism or success, is it?

2. Aggression

When needs aren't met, some people become aggressive in either their attitude, their behavior, or both. They may take exception to what is said and act increasingly confrontational. Or they may fall unusually quiet, while pursuing a passive-aggressive approach. Otherwise mild-mannered people who become uncharacteristically aggressive may also be highly unpredictable. You can't anticipate their next action because they don't know it themselves.

3. Rationalization

My favorite definition of *rationalize* is this: "to rationalize is to tell 'rational lies.'" Let's break it down:

- Rational: logical, reasonable, sensible, acceptable
- Lies: fabrications, deceptions, falsehoods, untruths

When needs are unmet, we start telling ourselves logical, acceptable, reasonable untruths. Then we choose to believe these deceptions and act like they are true. Put a different way: people with unmet needs may create an alternate reality that seems comfortable enough to them. Take one more look at those three predictable responses again. Do you see it? Interestingly, the acronym for responses to unmet needs is WAR.

The **WAR** of Unmet Needs: Withdrawal. Aggression. Rationalization.

When your needs, my needs, or anyone else's needs aren't satisfied, we're in a battle—a WAR. But we are not defenseless. Prepared in advance with a sharply honed emotional intelligence, we can more quickly recognize and rectify the behaviors that would otherwise sabotage our professional survival and success.

Ideas to Accelerate My Success

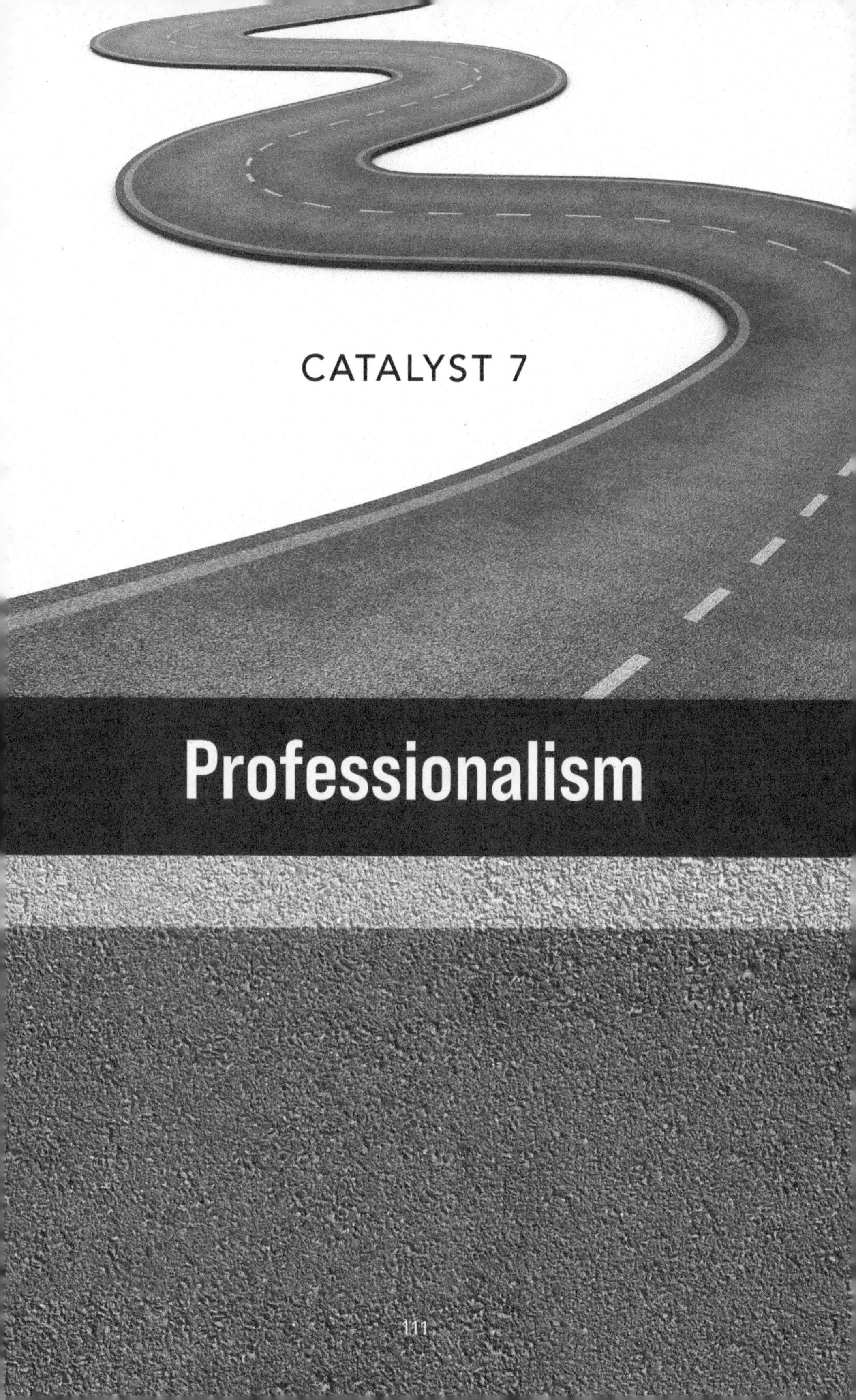

CATALYST 7

Professionalism

CHAPTER 19

Service with a "Capital" S

"Professional success is always rooted in the ability to offer service to others, coupled with an unfailing willingness to act." —PHILLIP VAN HOOSER

Several years ago, I was in Georgia speaking to a group of country club managers. After my leadership training session, one of the participants shared a story involving one of his team members, Bob. Interestingly, he began his story with an apology.

"I'm sorry, Phil, but this story is about service, not leadership." But as it turned out, he had nothing to apologize for.

He explained the occasion in question occurred during an exceptionally busy holiday weekend at his Capital City Club in downtown Atlanta. It seems a club member and his guests approached the bar, where they were greeted warmly by Bob, the club's head bartender.

Bob began the process of taking and filling drink orders until one of the guests ordered a specialty drink. Bob paused, apologized, and explained he was unfamiliar with that particular drink. However, he said that if the guest could provide the ingredients, he would do his best to fill the gentlemen's order.

"Well, that's my problem," the guest explained. "While visiting New Orleans recently, I stayed at the Fairmont Hotel, where someone recommended the specialty of the house—a Sazerac. I only remember the name because the bar and the drink were the same. Anyway, I ordered the Sazerac and loved it. But since then, every time I've tried to order it elsewhere, I've gotten the same reaction as I just got from you. I was just hoping a place like the Capital City Club might be different. But don't worry about it—I'll just have a Bloody Mary instead."

Bob worked quickly and professionally to prepare and serve the guest's alternate order. With Bloody Mary in hand, the guest rejoined his host's party.

At the same time, Bob voluntarily abandoned his post at the bar in search of a telephone. He was soon speaking directly with the bartender on duty at—are you ready for this—The Sazerac Bar at the Fairmont Hotel in New Orleans, Louisiana.

Now imagine, if you will, the scene just a few minutes later when Bob, the Capital City Club bartender, approaches the guest's table. Imagine the guest's surprise, satisfaction, and ultimate delight when Bob says, "Excuse me sir, but here's the Sazerac you requested. I hope you'll find it to your liking. And sir, I've taken the liberty of writing down the ingredients on this index card so you can carry it with you in your future travels. I certainly hope you enjoy your time here at the Capital City Club. My pleasure to serve you."

WOW—I love that story! Because it's all about great service! Can you see the service—and what's more, professionalism—lessons contained in the story?

First, Bob acknowledged the existence of a customer's unsatisfied need. The person exhibited neither anger nor aggression. Still, Bob clearly recognized his disappointment and dissatisfaction.

Second, Bob didn't use his current "busy" status as an excuse or a smokescreen to avoid doing just a little more for his customer. Initially, Bob wasn't sure he could satisfy this customer. But he was sure he could do something more—by doing something.

And in the end, everybody won. The guest was thrilled to have his specialty drink and its ingredients. Bob was heralded throughout the organization—by customers, management, and team members alike—as a "take charge," "can do," "get things done" professional who was more than ready to serve others.

And the Capital City Club? It solidified its reputation as a premier organization based solely on the quality of performance by its associates—in this case, Bob, the bartender.

Professional success is always rooted in the ability to offer service to others, coupled with an unfailing willingness to act. That's what I call service with a "Capital" S!

Ideas to Accelerate My Success

CHAPTER 20

The High Cost of Assumptions

"Treating everyone you meet with honor, respect, and dignity makes consistent, compounding contributions to your success ledger that you can bank on!" —Phillip Van Hooser

By now you know lessons on success can be found in a lot of different places. Today it's a story. And this one is important because it highlights the high cost of wrong assumptions.

The construction of Kentucky Dam and Kentucky Lake brought electricity to thousands of western Kentuckians in the 1930s and 40s. It also brought success and substantial wealth to at least one hard-scrabble western Kentucky farmer. His name was Clyde Reed.

In the early years of the dam's construction, Mr. Reed took a risk that paid off handsomely. Recognizing the lake construction would require millions of tons of limestone rock, and well aware his farm was perfectly positioned atop a huge limestone deposit in close proximity to the lake project, Clyde Reed acted.

The Reed farm soon became a limestone quarry, and Reed Crushed Stone Company was founded. In the years that followed, hundreds of millions of dollars of revenue were realized.

Although financially secure, Mr. Reed never relinquished his "common man" roots and practical sensibilities. Favoring khaki work clothes and boots rather than a suit and tie, Mr. Reed often sat outside company headquarters planning his next business deal—all the while waving at neighbors as they drove past.

One day a young salesman pulled into the company parking lot for his first visit. As he stepped from his vehicle, an old man sitting in the shade greeted him.

"Mornin' son. What brings you to Lake City, Kentucky, today?"

"I'm here to meet Clyde Reed," was the salesman's somewhat curt reply.

The old man—Mr. Reed himself—chose not to reveal his identity at that point. Instead. he asked, "So what're you sellin' the old man?"

Marginally frustrated, the young salesman replied, "I sell huge earth-moving equipment—each costing more than $100,000 per unit."

He handed the old man a brochure, hoping to avoid more questions. It worked. The old man reviewed the brochure carefully before eventually speaking again. "Son, I like the looks of these. Why don't you write up an order for four of 'em?"

An awkward silence settled over the conversation. For the salesman, this irritating little game had gone on long enough.

"Sir, I don't have any more time for you," he said, retrieving his brochure. And I told you I have an important meeting with Clyde Reed."

With that, the young man turned and headed inside, unaware his meeting with Mr. Reed had already begun.

Now try to imagine the young salesman's shock when the receptionist acknowledged Mr. Reed's entrance a few minutes later. Of course, the young salesman apologized profusely. But Mr. Reed stopped him.

"Son, no need to apologize. Just come on into my office."

Once inside, Mr. Reed continued, "Now son, go ahead and write up that order like I asked before. But know I'll be calling your boss to tell him this sale is contingent on you not receiving even one penny of commission for it. Son, I hope you understand. You don't take people for granted—if you do, it can cost you."

Here's the lesson for professionals: successful professionals—regardless of their position, title, or status—simply can't afford to make and act upon unfounded assumptions about customers, team members, colleagues, or associates.

And assumptions are so easy to make. First impressions—appearance, accents, dress, age, sex—the list can go on and on.

But what happens if your assumption is wrong?

As we've already learned here, a bad assumption can cost you—a lot! However, treating everyone you meet with honor, respect, and dignity—even when they prove themselves unworthy of the same—makes consistent, compounding contributions to your success ledger that you can bank on!

Ideas to Accelerate My Success

_____

_____

_____

_____

_____

_____

_____

_____

_____

_____

_____

_____

_____

_____

_____

_____

_____

_____

_____

_____

_____

_____

_____

CATALYST 8

Teamwork

CHAPTER 21

Building Trust with a Multigenerational Workforce

"Successful professionals build trust by delivering on everything, every time." —ALYSON VAN HOOSER

When people trust you, they will listen, learn, follow, and grow with you long-term. Building trust in a multigenerational world requires intentional focus. There are subjects you should and should not talk about, questions you should and should not ask, and actions you must absolutely take.

So how do you know what to do for whom? I know it can seem like the differences between generations are endless, but from experiencing situations both on the team leader and the associate side of the equation, I think we are more similar than different. When I worked in the retail and finance industries, I used these three tips to build trust across multigenerational groups of people. They are practical, specific, and they work. Here we go!

Talk Up, Not Down

Think of your organizational chart. There are subjects you can discuss with the people above you, and there are things you should never discuss with the people below you. One example: individual performance. When it comes to performance, talk up, not down.

Let's pretend you are supervising a poor-performing frontline associate named Gary. Do not discuss Gary's poor performance with Gary's peers. That conversation should only be had with Gary in private or with your supervisor if absolutely necessary. Talk *up* the organizational chart, not *down*.

If you open up to Gary's peers in that way, you may feel like you are building a deeper relationship with them. Instead, you are breaking their level of trust and confidence in you. They wonder—if you will talk negatively about Gary with them, will you also talk negatively about them to someone else? Once they lose trust, then you lose their buy-in. Should you listen to Gary's peers if they complain about him? Absolutely. But listen only—don't add to the complaint.

No matter our generation, we all want a team leader whom we can trust not to talk bad about us to our peers.

Don't Ask Their Opinion Unless...

As a new, young team leader, I thought it would be a great idea to ask all my seasoned team members and co-workers their opinions on projects I was working on. I thought this would provide insight for me, engage them, and help them feel more valued.

I was surprised one morning when my co-worker became frustrated because I asked his opinion on one of my new projects. Without hesitation, he said to me he had been giving me his opinion over and over, but I never take it! Regardless of my intent, he didn't feel more valued; he felt devalued. He was not more engaged; he was more distant. He didn't trust his opinion even mattered to me. I had to apologize to him.

You can build trust with people—co-workers or customers—by asking their opinion. But don't ask their opinion unless you will actually consider it. Don't ask their opinion unless you are going to explain your final decision. Don't ask their opinion unless you are clear about your intention in asking them.

No matter our generation, we all want to feel our opinion is valued.

Deliver on Everything

Have you ever had someone promise something but not deliver? No matter how big or small, when people do not deliver on their word, others lose trust in them. Here is a real-world example.

There was a sales contest in another department of the business. The contributor with the highest sales at the end of six weeks would win a $50 Visa gift card. The person who won the contest never received the gift card. Even years after that contest, the associate never forgot that their supervisor didn't deliver on the gift card promise. They also spread the word around the office every time new contests were announced.

How do you think that affected team morale and motivation? It was bad. No one was motivated to push for higher success because they couldn't trust that their supervisor would deliver.

If you make a promise to your team or to a customer, you better deliver. If you tell your people that you are going to do a 360° review, do it. If you say you will have a project done by a certain date, deliver on it. If you say you'll get back to a customer at a certain time, don't be late. Successful professionals build trust by delivering on everything, every time.

And every generation appreciates that.

Ideas to Accelerate My Success

CHAPTER 22

Wow Them with Your Weakness

"Set the example for your people to recognize weaknesses and use them to intentionally improve performance." —ALYSON VAN HOOSER

Many people still believe in the *never let them see you sweat* mentality. And there are situations where I'd agree. But at other times, it could be that this vulnerability is what starts the shift toward radical success in your life.

I was working with a group that was trying to build a stronger culture of unity and teamwork. From my observations, the disconnect between decision-makers and team members in the organization was just big enough to stall major progress toward their culture goal for years to come.

In order for a culture shift to happen in an organization, those at the top have to set the example of the new expectation.

Beth, a key leader on the team, was unmatched when it came to technical skills, but her people skills were lacking. The way she interacted with some team members—or didn't interact at all with others—communicated the message that a unified team was nice in theory but not something those at the top actually wanted on a daily basis. Some associates said she was one to "talk the talk but not walk the walk." People believe what they see. Beth's colleagues felt that she didn't seem to want the unified culture of teamwork they'd heard her talk about so often. The disconnect between her words and her actions was a clear reason why progress toward the organization's culture transformation was gridlocked.

The interesting thing is that Beth knew her interpersonal skills were weak. (Typically, it takes a while to get people to see and admit their own weaknesses!) Beth told me straight up she was uncomfortable talking one on one with people she didn't know well. And because it would make her so anxious, she avoided going to certain departments in the organization or would make time for only a quick drop-by to say hello.

The dynamics of the leader/team member relationship are critical in all cases, but especially when you are working to create to a stronger culture of teamwork. Beth had to do something about her weak interpersonal skills. It was the largest stone blocking the organization's path to reaching their goal. After careful planning, Beth agreed to admit her weakness to the entire team. Why would she do this? Here are three reasons.

Be the Self-Awareness Example

We all have strengths and weaknesses. Understanding those characteristics is key to individual and team success. Try as you might to hide them, it's likely that everyone else already knows your weaknesses as a team member. So, although your weaknesses are not news to your colleagues, sharing them shows your team that you're not oblivious. This gives you an opportunity to set the example for your people to recognize their own weaknesses and intentionally improve their performance.

Earn Yourself Grace

People are more likely to extend grace to you when they know you're working to get better at something. Beth was uncomfortable talking with people she didn't know. She admitted it. So, when she came around and tried to start a conversation with someone—even if it was awkward at first—they showed her grace and simply loved that she was trying! They also struck up good working conversations with Beth because they knew that was her area of weakness. How do I know this? They told me!

Admitting your weakness may not be easy for you. It's a humbling step to take. But when you're humble, you earn grace from people—customers and co-workers alike. You earn the opportunity to show up in a way that might not be perfect.

As things change in your life and at work, mistakes will happen. To continue making forward progress, showing grace to one another is key to creating an environment where people can try and succeed—but also try and "fail up."

Make Them Say "Wow!"

Oftentimes people try to keep up with an expectation that they must be polished and perfect. But to be honest, that doesn't impress many people these days. People want real—they want authentic leaders and co-workers!

You can "wow" people with your weakness. Admitting your weaknesses shows you are not perfect—no one is. People won't think you're weak because they no longer see you as perfect. Instead, they'll think, *Wow…that person is self-aware, humble, brave, and someone we want to work with and get behind.*

Turn over a New Leaf

Just as I expected, after that tough conversation on Beth's part, progress really began to pick up in the organization. It's true—humble, self-aware people who communicate well and set the example for what they expect will always be the ones with the highest likelihood of achieving success. Maybe it's time; maybe you have a reason strong enough to finally let them see you sweat. It could be one of the best decisions you make.

Ideas to Accelerate My Success

_____

_____

_____

_____

CHAPTER 23

The Power of Empowerment

"Empowerment is the practical process of willingly and knowingly granting your official power to another." —PHILLIP VAN HOOSER

My professional journey began with the dawning of the 1980s. And what a volatile time it was!

The U.S. inflation rate peaked at 14.76 percent in April 1980. Correspondingly, the Federal Funds Rate skyrocketed to an almost unbelievable 20 percent that same year! By 1982, the United States was mired in the worst recession since the Great Depression of the 1930s. Massive numbers of businesses, farms, and homes were lost due to default or foreclosure. Unemployment soared to a national average of 10.8 percent, with some individual states exceeding a 16 percent unemployment rate.

And just when it looked like things couldn't get any worse—they did! In 1987, the world's financial barometer—the U.S. stock market—crashed, and with it, fear and uncertainty were exported around the globe.

And that's the period in which yours truly began his business career. Interestingly, I learned even in the midst of business misfortune and professional mayhem, opportunities to learn and grow still exist.

Fortunately, forward-looking business owners, entrepreneurs, and business professionals of all kinds existed then, as now—professionals committed not only to surviving perilous times, but to building sustainable businesses that are prepared and equipped to thrive in any environment. But building versatile, adaptable, responsive businesses requires enlisting and harvesting the creativity, imagination, and brain power of every team member, associate, and contributor—at every level.

In many ways, the economic desperation of the 1980s provided a much-needed, long-overdue jumpstart to empowering teams as never before.

To fully understand the concept of empowerment, you have to begin by accepting *power*, the root word from which empowerment is derived. Power in practice is essentially the ability grant, withhold, or withdraw something someone wants or needs. Of course, there's more—much more—that could be said about the proper—and improper—use of power. But at the moment, our focus is specifically on empowerment. Empowerment is the practical process of willingly and knowingly granting your official power to another.

Forward-thinking professionals are quick to recognize the many benefits associated with empowered team members. But many don't know where to start. And others still wonder, "Is the juice worth the squeeze?"

Trust is at the heart of any successful empowerment initiative. Before you, me, or anyone can freely empower another person, we must trust their level of commitment to be consistent with our own. We must trust the person to be adequately educated, trained, skilled, and motivated to make and implement quality decisions. And we must trust the person's objectives are rightly aligned with those of the organization.

If and when sufficient levels of trust are established, empowerment can become a reality. However, if trust is absent, empowerment is more a mental exercise than a practical reality.

So how can you get from here to there? With these steps: PREPARE. SHARE. DECLARE.

Mindful business pros seek out opportunities to *prepare* those around them.

Once adequately prepared, these same business professionals willingly *share* their vested power with individuals who are mentally and emotionally ready to accept the challenges ahead.

Finally, once the power has been shared, professionals definitively *declare* their support and confidence in their trusted—and now empowered—associates. (For further guidance, download the Six Levels of Empowerment guide at https://www.vanhooser.com/employee-empowerment/.)

I once heard someone say that "tough times don't last—but tough people do." The 1980s taught me something different. I learned the tougher the times, the more necessary empowerment is. Power, trust, preparation, communication, empowerment—these are concepts successful business professionals know...and practice.

Ideas to Accelerate My Success

CATALYST 9

Leading

CHAPTER 24

The Recipe for Respect

"There are no shortcuts to respect. You have to earn it!" —PHILLIP VAN HOOSER

Apparently, some things need to be spelled out to emphasize their significance. Here's an example.

Way back in 1967, noted rhythm and blues singer Aretha Franklin covered a song written and recorded earlier by the late, great Otis Redding. The words and tune were essentially the same on both recordings, with one noteworthy exception. Aretha's version spelled out—literally and figuratively—what she was singing about. Her version became a huge hit and, ultimately, the signature song of her illustrious career. And all it took was seven letters—punctuated by a declarative statement. Do you remember? "R-E-S-P-E-C-T—find out what it means to me."

Otis and Aretha had their way of earning respect, but let me make one thing perfectly clear: Contrary to what others would have you believe, respect is not some possession to be acquired or some crown to be bestowed. And respect is not assigned based on age, sex, education, status, intelligence, seniority, title, or any other similar concept. There are no shortcuts to be had if you want to experience the personal satisfaction that comes with truly being respected by others. Business professionals still acquire respect the old-fashioned way—they earn it! And to earn respect, it helps to know the recipe and ingredients.

The first ingredient is **consistency**.

Believe me, successful professionals never take consistency for granted. They recognize that team members and associates spend an inordinate amount of time watching, listening, and carefully evaluating even the most subtle comments, actions, and motivations they make. From these personal observations, team members begin to determine whether or not a person is to be respected. Consistency contributes to respect.

The second ingredient is **quality decision-making**.

Note, I stress *quality* decision-making, not *flawless* decision-making. Why the distinction? To be flawless in decision-making requires a person to possess perfect knowledge of the future. Of course, no such crystal ball exists. Thankfully, the ability to make sound, reasonable decisions in a thoughtful, timely manner is a skill that can be developed by virtually any person. High-quality decisions deepen respect.

Finally, the third ingredient is **the ability to interact well with others**.

Respect doesn't germinate in a vacuum. For both respect—and professionalism—to take root and grow, business professionals, owners, and entrepreneurs must have continuing opportunities to interact with other people. Shortsighted people who consciously choose to disassociate or limit contact with their team members and colleagues are foolishly allowing the fertile soil where healthy relationships grow to erode. Interacting well with people increases respect.

I've carefully spelled out the recipe for earning respect: consistency and quality decision-making, coupled with thoughtful interactions with other people. Apply and tend to these ingredients, and soon earned respect from others moves from concept to reality. R-E-S-P-E-C-T—now you know what it means to me...and what it will do for you!

Ideas to Accelerate My Success

_____

_____

_____

_____

_____

_____

_____

_____

_____

_____

_____

_____

_____

CHAPTER 25

Developing Strategic Leaders

"Where are you right now? The answer should establish a baseline from which your personal strategic growth plans can be made." —PHILLIP VAN HOOSER

If you've served as a business leader in almost any organization, you're likely familiar with the process of strategic planning. If you've somehow avoided such exposure until now, your time has come!

I want to introduce you to my philosophy of strategic planning as it applies to business professionals and pose a specific strategic question for your consideration. Then I'll challenge you to craft answers for that question as it applies to you.

Let's begin with understanding what strategic planning is. Strategic planning is a process that organizations use to define their strategy or direction and then make decisions on how to allocate resources to accomplish desired end goals. In other words, a strategic plan is intended to determine how the ends or goals will be achieved by the means or resources available.

And guess what? Strategic planning is not just a tool to be used by organizations. Strategic planning works well for business professionals, entrepreneurs, team members, and individuals too—people just like you.

Here's how. Consider this defining strategic question: *Where am I right now?*

This foundational question is critical to establish a baseline from which your personal strategic growth plans will be made.

But here's the key—you must be honest with yourself. And the honest answer to "Where am I right now?" involves far more than where you work, what you do there, and how long you've been doing it.

In the big scheme of things, your employer, title, and seniority have very little to do with who you really are as a business professional. Instead, to effectively determine where you are right now, you need to carefully evaluate your capabilities, opportunities, and expectations. To do that, answer these additional questions.

1. What are my strengths?

Are you organized? Decisive? Composed under pressure? Confident? Don't be unnecessarily modest here. If you can do it, go ahead and list it. Remember, this list is for your eyes only.

2. What are my weaknesses?

Again, honesty is critical. What don't you do very well? Are you a poor communicator? Are you inconsistent in your decision-making? Do you procrastinate? Do you have a reputation for being unable to control your emotions?

3. What opportunities are available to enhance my professional skills?

This book might be one. What about available online classes to help shore up your weaknesses? Are you diligent in staying current with your professional reading? Is there someone who could coach or mentor you?

4. What threats exist if I don't continue to develop as a professional?

I know, this is a tough question. It needs to be. You need to consider if it's possible that the expanding responsibilities of your position could eventually outpace your professional skill set. Is it possible that someone could lead your team more effectively than you—either now or in the future? Is it possible that your position and responsibilities could be taken from you and given to another? As difficult as it may be, you need to consider such worst-case scenarios as a proactive measure.

So now you have some work to do. If it would help, read this chapter one more time. Then go to work answering the questions. Don't stop now. I promise you, the strategic work you do today will serve you well in the future. So get started!

Ideas to Accelerate My Success

_____

_____

_____

_____

_____

_____

_____

_____

_____

_____

_____

_____

_____

_____

_____

_____

_____

_____

_____

_____

_____

_____

_____

_____

CHAPTER 26

Stories, Not Statistics

*"When it comes to understanding how best
to connect with other people, stories tell you
what statistics can't."* —ALYSON VAN HOOSER

Strategies you've heard that promise to help business professionals recruit, retain, and lead great teams—but allow
no room for individual customization—likely won't work with
the current and future workforce and customer base.

Why? Because of the immediate access we have to job
opportunities, products, and services, and the diverse interests
and outcomes that today's workforce demands. Empirical evidence suggests those who take an individual approach to lead
their team and serve their customers will ultimately be much
more successful than those who don't.

So, how can you know *how* to interact with *whom*? When
it comes to understanding how best to connect with other
people, stories tell you what statistics can't. Stories capture
attention, stories are memorable, and stories are personal.

Stories break down barriers and build bonds. Stories unlock answers to challenges leaders like you must overcome. Stories connect a person to a brand, not just a product. To hire the right people, attract the right customers, and get them both to stay, start by learning these three stories about your people.

Defining Stories

Unless something extremely significant happens, most of us show up in a way that is shaped by what we experienced growing up. When we were young, we learned how to build relationships, respond to rejection, achieve success, get what we want, deal with conflict, work as a team, and more.

When it comes to your team at work, you might talk with your people about how they learned their work ethic. My husband learned from his dad showing up and working hard—even when it's not convenient—will earn you experience, success, and respect. If one of your team members grew up learning a strong work ethic and realizing the benefits, it's a safe assumption they'll show up with a strong work ethic throughout their time in the workforce, too.

On the other hand, I grew up with parents who did not work. I saw, felt, and lived the negative effects of that. I never want that for myself or my family. If you have a team member who was dealt a tough hand and they overcame it, it's likely they'll continue that same positive trajectory going forward.

Imagine for a moment that you are interviewing a potential candidate. You ask them how they learned their work ethic and the interviewee has no response. Would this be a red flag from a dependability or performance perspective? Think about it.

When you understand a team member's past, you are in a better position to predict and prepare for how they will act in the future.

When it comes to customers, asking them where they learned their work ethic could potentially open up the conversation to reveal what type of work ethic they expect from you to do business—or keep doing business—with you. How much more successful would you be if you consistently met that expectation with all your diverse customers? It might not be easy, but earning success rarely ever is!

Today's Heartbeat

Many organizations do exit interviews. Fewer have implemented the valuable tool of "stay interviews." It's important for business owners and company professionals to know what keeps a team member showing up and giving their best.

If you lead a team, you might ask a team member what a perfect day in their work life would look like. One associate may quickly tell you they would come in, keep their head down, do their job, not hear from anyone, and leave on time. Another team member might say they'd want to be involved in many different projects, interact with lots of different people, and wrap the day meeting with you one on one to discuss progress. Ultimately, you may hear little nuggets from your people about when, how, or what they need from you.

When it comes to your customers, the next time you're having a conversation with them, ask them why they stay with you. You might learn it's because of price. Maybe you'll learn it's because you have their favorite product. It's possible they might be staying just because of you!

When you understand why your people stay, you're better positioned to never have to watch them leave.

American Dreams

Do you know where you and your people want to be in one, five, or ten years? If you haven't had a conversation about this in the past, now would be a great time.

For team leaders, ask your people to describe what success will look like to them in ten years. Someone may surprise you and say they picture themselves as an entrepreneur. You need to know if someone is not in it for the long haul. Another person may tell you they want to be a leader in a different department in the organization. There's your sign you should start giving them opportunities to grow, as well as making time to develop their replacement when they get promoted.

When you're serving customers, think about all the innovative ideas you could implement, all the customers you might keep and attract, if you become what they already know they're going to want in the future. You're securing your future success by asking them how they picture their future!

When you understand the destination, you can make plans to take roads to get there faster, better, and stronger.

The One Time You Should Talk Before You Listen

If you've ever been in our leadership development training, you know we emphasize how critical it is for you to listen first. However, this may be the one time I suggest you should actually talk first.

People are more willing to share personal, insightful stories with people they trust. Before you jump straight into asking your people about *their* stories, start by sharing yours. When you intentionally open up to people about your life, they'll feel *you* trust *them* more. In turn, they'll be more likely to feel *they* can trust *you*, too. And stories of trust are what every successful leader wants more of!

Ideas to Accelerate My Success

CHAPTER 27

LEGOs, Leadership, and Leveling Up

"Engagement, not involvement, is the secret to effective leadership." —ALYSON VAN HOOSER

Willow and Lincoln, my two oldest, are often asked to play with Duke, their three-year-old brother, while I work at home. The toy of choice in our house is LEGOs—we have hundreds of them. The bigger kids love them, so it's the go-to activity when they are on "Duke duty." As Duke plays with the big kids, I hope he will learn to build, learn bigger words, and learn to play well with others. I also hope the time they spend together builds a solid foundation for their relationships.

Imagine the kids all at the table with hundreds of tiny building blocks. Do you know what happens when a three-year-old sees a tall house freshly built by his brother or sister? Well, I can tell you, he doesn't stand back in awe. Quite the opposite. Picture a *threenager* using his arm like Thor's hammer and emitting noises that make you think a T-Rex has come to life. Then, as LEGOs come crashing down under the force of a toddler on a mission, without fail, the next sound I hear in older sibling unison is, "MOM!"

Immediately, I know what's happened. Willow and Lincoln have involved Duke, but they have not engaged Duke. Here's what I mean.

Involving Versus Engaging

Involving someone looks like all three kids sitting at the table, each with their own pile of LEGOs. Likely, the older two are building something with each other. Duke, happy to simply be at the table with them, is building by himself. He will look frequently at what they're doing. But if he tries to help, he's quickly redirected or ignored. Eventually, Duke will get tired of being on the outside…involved but not engaged. That's when we have the Thor/T-Rex situation.

When someone is only involved, not engaged, it's a no-win situation for everyone. However, both involving and engaging someone makes for a very different experience and result.

Involving *and* engaging looks like all the kids playing LEGOs again, but this time they invite Duke to play a real part in their building process. They ask Duke what he thinks they should build; then they listen and consider his suggestions. When Duke asks "why" a million times, they patiently answer his questions. They encourage Duke to put LEGOs on the building, even if it means they eventually have to do more work to fix it.

When both involved and engaged, Duke learns how to play and build better. He has more fun, which means they play together longer. And ultimately, Willow and Lincoln have made little deposits into their relationship banks with Duke, which will reap benefits for their entire life. It's a win-win for everyone!

Two Tips to Involve and Engage

Often in organizations, well-intentioned leaders involve team members, but they don't reap valuable results because they don't also engage them. If you want your people to perform better and you want to create more respect and loyalty among your team members, use these two actions to involve and engage them.

1. Invite more people to important meetings.

Sure, most people wouldn't be excited to attend another meeting, but high performers probably would! The opportunity to learn beyond their current role is a big deal to associates looking to capitalize on opportunities.

Is there an aspect of your business some team members would benefit from understanding better? Invite them to a meeting. And don't just invite them and make them sit on the sidelines. Instead, let them play with *your LEGOs*. Let them build with you, not merely near you. Welcome questions, not silence. Be the leader who identifies people with potential and engages them in experiences to help them grow.

2. Give increased responsibility; then encourage your people to try and fail.

It can be hard to trust someone who hasn't yet proven their ability to complete a job or big project successfully. But just like a smart toddler, a person may surprise you with their success.

On the other hand, the person very well may fail. Duke may put the wrong size LEGO in the wrong spot or accidentally knock something over while trying to help. But after he recognizes the mistake, he will work to fix it. And it's unlikely he will intentionally make the same mistake again. End result: He becomes a stronger part of the team.

Failure stings, but pain is one of the best teachers. Be the leader who creates increasingly strong relationships because you appreciate failed attempts to deliver positive results—which are sure to come!

> "The most successful leaders understand true leadership is serving others."

Level Up Your Leadership

The most successful leaders understand true leadership is serving others. Involving and engaging your people is an act of service—one that takes serious time and effort. But this act of service will improve your team, your level of customer service, and your success.

I encourage you to take your leadership to the next level by both involving and engaging people better. It starts first with a little assessment:

- Who on your team is not involved?
- Who on your team is involved but not actively engaged?

And don't forget about your customers! Which of your customers are not engaged? The more they're engaged with you, your products, and your service, the more likely they'll be to continue working with you!

Once you know who is where, work to bring everyone up to involved-and-engaged status. This is where you all will reap the benefits!

Ideas to Accelerate My Success

_____
_____
_____
_____
_____
_____
_____
_____
_____
_____
_____

CATALYST 10

Balance

CHAPTER 28

Success Balanced in Seasons

"Work-life balance is not trying to do it all—all the time. It's trying to do what is most important in each season of life." —ALYSON VAN HOOSER

In 2019, I wrote a book titled *Level Up: Elevate Your Game & Crush Your Goals*. In 2020, I had to take a big dose of my own medicine.

All through my 20s, I pushed to get where I could really follow my dreams. And the truth is, I was realizing success fast. But then, like lots of other people in the heart of the 2020 pandemic, I felt like the reality of success had been ripped from my future. At some point, maybe even right now, you might find yourself feeling this way.

There's a method I talk about in my book called "Lay Down the Law." It's the process I use to best understand myself, prioritize my goals, and continually make progress toward success.

During the pandemic, my priorities had to radically change. Ultimately, I had to redefine success for myself in that season of life. I went from prioritizing attempts to make huge moves professionally to ensuring I supported my four children physically, emotionally, and educationally through a pandemic. My professional career had to take a backseat.

Did that mean I was no longer successful or that I won't be successful in the future? To me, no. And if your experience is similar, it doesn't mean you can't be successful either.

First, only you can define success for yourself. For you, success may be financial freedom, or ultimate flexibility, or creating a safe, inviting environment in your home—you get to decide what success means for you.

I've realized balancing success must be done in seasons because the definition changes over time. Realizing this has helped me understand what true work-life balance is. It's not trying to do it all—all the time. Rather, it's trying to do what is most important in each season of life.

These questions help me balance success in different seasons. They may be helpful for you to ask yourself, too.

1. What are the three most important things for me to achieve in my current season?

Prior to the pandemic, I had more time to focus on my professional goals because my kids were in school and doing extracurricular activities. During the pandemic, most of my time was spent taking care of a newborn and helping my other kids navigate virtual school.

I'm going to be transparent. During the pandemic, my goals were to ensure my kids, my husband, and I stayed emotionally healthy; to ensure my kids didn't regress in their education; and to maintain my career through this pandemic. I decided that if I could accomplish those three things, I would be successful.

As I am writing this, we're coming out of the pandemic. It's time for a realignment. I get to reprioritize my time—to rebalance success in this new season of life.

What are your top three priorities in your current stage of life? Once you've defined them, allocate appropriate time to making yourself successful in all of them.

2. If I am currently in or about to go through a season shift, how will I show up differently for the people around me? And how do I need them to show up for me?

When I say "show up," I mean how will you be a part of someone's life? Will you interact with them every day, maybe once a week, maybe only if there's an emergency? There are all kinds of ways we can show up for people—phone calls and texts, going out together, attending important events together, or being on-call when needed.

During the pandemic, I was emotionally spent. I could not show up for friends in the way I did before. After all was said and done with my family, I had very little left for myself or anyone else.

Good communication is vital in every aspect of our lives. It's how we create unified, strong relationships, which add such richness to our journey. I had to tell my friends where I was emotionally. I had to ask them where they were. Then we had to adapt how we interacted...how we showed up for each other. We talked and hung out less, but we knew we were always there for each other, even if we were less a part of each other's daily routines.

As you move forward to achieve success in your current reality, will you have to show up differently for your people? If so, tell them. If they love you, they'll cheer you on to crush your goals and be at the finish line with you when you do. And if you need them to show up differently for you, talk with them about how they can do that.

3. When will the season change?

Sometimes it's hard to say. But this is key: you have to know where you're going so that you know when you've arrived. If you're planning for a family, starting a side hustle, anticipating a career change, or beginning a bucket-list project—if you're adding or shifting priorities in your life—during that new season you're going to be adding more tasks that will take up your time. Some tasks may take every waking minute you have, while other things can be added without much shift needed in your schedule.

Achieving success is undoubtedly a balancing act. You have to look at the full picture of your life so you can plan your success through the various seasons you will experience. Understanding what you want your life to look like over the next few years will help you find better balance. You will have seasons where you spend more time pouring into your career, others where you pour more into your family, others where you pour more into your community or church. Balance is achieved in seasons, and anticipating the next season will help give you clarity and peace in the balancing act.

Achieving Balance

As you work to achieve success in this season, maybe now is the perfect time for you to shift priorities or add a different priority to your life. Or maybe now isn't the right season for change, but you realize that season is not too far off. Wherever you find yourself, go all in, because we all know seasons don't last very long. Soon enough rain will turn to snow, then snow to sunshine. When you get the opportunity to look back, make sure you can say that you made the best of it.

Ideas to Accelerate My Success

_____

_____

_____

_____

_____

_____

CHAPTER 29

The Positive "No"

"When you leave people with alternatives, you leave them with hope." —PHILLIP VAN HOOSER

Y ou're minding your own business when your phone rings. On the line is a friend, family member, business associate, or possibly a total stranger. Whomever it is, it's unmistakable—they want something from you. It could be your money, your time, your effort, maybe even your influence. Whatever it is, you quickly know you have no interest in participating. It's that simple.

But then it gets complicated. You realize everything you say or do could potentially impact your professional image and future opportunities. So, what now? How do you say "no" without burning bridges?

Most of us have stumbled through a similar situation. We say things like, "Well, that sounds interesting. Let me think more about it. Can I get back to you in a few days?"

The caller is fueled by anticipation of an affirmative response, but you know differently. You know you're not going to participate. You just don't know how to say "no" in a positive, nondestructive way.

When facing such pressure, try practicing the "positive 'no.'" It's a simple, straightforward, and effective technique that can be accomplished in five easy steps.

1. **Listen intently to the complete thought, idea, suggestion, or request.** Promising opportunities have been missed by tuning others out prematurely. Stay focused. Great ideas can come from anyone, anywhere, anytime.

2. **Consciously determine your level of interest and involvement.** Once you've heard the proposition in question, determine if you want to participate. Be honest with yourself—is this opportunity right for you?

3. **If you're not interested, say so quickly and definitively.** Keep this in mind: for those who will understand your decision, no in-depth explanation is necessary; for those who will not understand your decision, no in-depth explanation will suffice.

4. **Provide alternative solutions.** You're able to make virtually any negative more positive by offering viable alternatives. Here's how: "No, John, I won't be taking advantage of your offer at this point, but have you considered…" Then list reasonable alternatives for their consideration and action. When you leave people with alternatives, you leave them with hope. And hope is good. I'm positive about that!

Ideas to Accelerate My Success

_____

_____

_____

_____

_____

_____

_____

_____

_____

_____

_____

_____

_____

_____

_____

_____

_____

_____

_____

_____

_____

_____

_____

_____

_____

_____

_____

_____

CHAPTER 30

Stay Grounded in the Grind

"In the pursuit of productivity, we miss our purpose." —ALYSON VAN HOOSER

I don't believe anybody's true purpose in life is to serve themselves. Instead, I think our purpose is rooted in serving others. It's a life well lived, full of meaning, contentment, and no regrets when we use our gifts and calling to achieve success through serving others.

But if we're not careful, we'll get wrapped up in "achieving" our purpose and completely lose sight of the object of our purpose—other people. It usually plays out like this...

We figure out our gifts and line them up with opportunities to serve. For example, I do that through speaking, training, and writing. You may do that through sharing products or services to help others achieve their goals, or teaching others about what you know, or using your gifts to help in someone else's business.

Then, in order to make sure we do those things well, we make lists of everything we must do. Productivity, right? We start tracking all our daily tasks—steps to accomplish the goal. And in the pursuit of productivity, we miss our purpose. Our priorities get out of balance.

How do you stay grounded in your purpose in the midst of the grind? Here are three ways. As you plan your to-do list, add these three action items so that at the end of the week— and over a lifetime—you've achieved more than just fill your own cup.

1. Celebrate Someone

There's always a reason to celebrate. Holidays, birthdays, and anniversaries are reasons, of course. But there are also national holidays like National Pizza Day. Who wouldn't love being surprised with free food?! You can celebrate summer break, a professional achievement, or simply *just because.*

Celebrating is all about reinforcing who and what is most important. For the person on the receiving end, it feels good to have someone reiterate that they are important. For you, it focuses your mind on selfless acts, which creates a much more meaningful existence.

2. Serve Someone

Everyone has hard things they're dealing with in their life. Pick someone—a co-worker, customer, friend, or family member—then think of a way to serve them. Clean their house, pick up their kids, buy their groceries—you get the idea.

Serving others is not about what's convenient for you. Serving others is about giving them a leg up when they're struggling. Whether you know them personally or not, who can you help this week?

3. Strengthen Someone

Empowering others is key to everyone living out their calling. How can you use your words, actions, time, and other resources to strengthen someone? Maybe you make time to speak life and encouragement into someone. It could mean you choose to say "yes" to the person who has asked you to mentor them—it's your turn to strengthen them with your knowledge. It could be a handwritten note that simply says, "I believe in you." How can you empower someone to live up to their full potential? Something as simple as that may help someone else turn a corner into a better, brighter future.

Grinding for the Greater Good

When we realize this life is not about *me*, but about *us*, helping each other crush personal goals, we all arrive in a better place. Keep your intentions pure, focus on serving others, and then the grind will be better balanced, because you're serving the greater good!

Ideas to Accelerate My Success

_____

_____

_____

_____

_____

_____

_____

_____

_____

_____

_____

_____

_____

_____

_____

_____

_____

_____

_____

_____

_____

_____

_____

What Have You Learned?

Roman Emperor Marcus Aurelius was born April 26th, 121 AD, and died March 17th, 180 AD. By the time of his death at age 59, he had ascended to the throne and was widely known as "The Philosopher King."

I'm going to do just a bit of personal philosophizing intended to make you think. But let's be honest—we both know that thinking and taking action can be two separate things entirely.

It is interesting that history remembers Marcus Aurelius less for his military achievements and more for his contemplative nature. For several years, Marcus Aurelius kept a personal notebook. Daily he dedicated time to considering, then recording, what he'd learned that day. His writings were never intended to make some grand point or to be a bestseller. It was simply one person undertaking a process of personal self-examination for the singular purpose of understanding himself, his way of life, and ultimately his actions.

Years after Marcus Aurelius's death, these written contemplations were discovered, then published under the title *The*

Meditations. Now, almost 2,000 years later, those meditations are still relevant to our learning.

Let me ask, do you possess a similar desire, curiosity, and courage to know yourself and your professional behavior better? Do you have the intellectual curiosity to explore new methods of becoming more successful? Or the professional courage to do things you've not done before—driven by the desire to make a lasting difference?

If so, ask yourself, *What have I learned from this book?*

I mean it. Literally, stop right now, take pen in hand, and capture recollections from what you've read.

But don't stop there. What about other professional experiences—good and bad? What have you learned from them? Have these experiences beneficially informed, or possibly changed, your thinking and actions since?

If so, congratulations! Good job! Keep learning, and keep growing!

But if not, why not? And what are you doing to ensure a better outcome in the future?

And while you're at it, ask yourself a second question: *What am I going to do to maintain the momentum that has been established?*

Everybody needs a plan, and everybody needs to commit to something. Commit to being diligent, single-minded, and undeterred in your pursuit of success.

Your team members, colleagues, customers, community, and your family deserve your best effort, and your effort shows itself in your personal commitment.

Let me paraphrase Marcus Aurelius: "Waste no more time arguing about what a successful professional should be... be one!"

Ideas to Accelerate My Success

About the Authors

Through the power of true connection, Alyson Van Hooser guides business professionals to engage authentically with people to radically improve performance and ignite high-caliber results! Alyson radiates an unexpected perspective on personal and professional success. Growing up in tough circumstances, she developed the emotional intelligence to "own" her way to uncommon success—including leading roles in big retail, banking, and city government—all before the age of 30! Her intuitive street smarts and ownership mindset show leaders, business owners, and professionals of all kinds how to unlock higher emotional intelligence and increased resilience to inspire and improve performance. A powerhouse keynote speaker, Alyson is an expert on employee engagement and performance and the author of *LEVEL UP: Elevate Your Game and Crush Your Goals.*

For 30+ years, top U.S. companies and organizations have trusted Phillip Van Hooser, MBA, CSP, CPAE, to show business professionals how to execute responsibilities while authentically connecting and engaging with people. As a result, thousands of people in hundreds of organizations have uncovered the real meaning of engaged leadership from the relatable, relevant illustrations and commonsense practices Phil uses. And in the process, they've discovered an arsenal of skills enabling them to achieve even greater personal and organizational results! A Hall of Fame keynote speaker, Phil is an expert on communication and leadership and the author of multiple business books, including *Earning the Right to Be Heard: Sell Your Ideas, Build Your Influence, Grow Your Opportunities*, *We Need to Talk: Building Trust When Communicating Gets Critical*, and *Leaders Ought to Know: 11 Ground Rules for Common Sense Leadership*.

Connect With Us

Let's stay connected! Find us on: in ▶ f ⊙

Or visit us at vanhooser.com for:

- Keynote presentations
- Leadership development training programs
- Executive coaching
- Online management courses
- More books, tools, and resources for success!

Van Hooser Associates, Inc.

vanhooser.com

hello@vanhooser.com

+1.270.365.1536

More Titles to Accelerate Your Success

Earning the Right to Be Heard: Sell Your Ideas, Build Your Influence, Grow Your Opportunities

Leaders Ought to Know: 11 Ground Rules for Common Sense Leadership

LEVEL UP: Elevate Your Game and Crush Your Goals

We Need to Talk: Building Trust When Communicating Gets Critical

Willie's Way: Six Secrets for Wooing, Wowing, and Winning Customers and Their Loyalty